BRING FORTH
the
LIGHT

EMMANUEL

BALBOA.
PRESS

A DIVISION OF HAY HOUSE

Balboa Press books may be ordered through booksellers or by contacting:

Balboa Press
A Division of Hay House
1663 Liberty Drive
Bloomington, IN 47403
www.balboapress.com
1-(877) 407-4847

Because of the dynamic nature of the Internet, any web addresses or links contained in this book may have changed since publication and may no longer be valid. The views expressed in this work are solely those of the author and do not necessarily reflect the views of the publisher, and the publisher hereby disclaims any responsibility for them.

The author of this book does not dispense medical advice or prescribe the use of any technique as a form of treatment for physical, emotional, or medical problems without the advice of a physician, either directly or indirectly. The intent of the author is only to offer information of a general nature to help you in your quest for emotional and spiritual well-being. In the event you use any of the information in this book for yourself, which is your constitutional right, the author and the publisher assume no responsibility for your actions.

Any people depicted in stock imagery provided by Thinkstock are models, and such images are being used for illustrative purposes only.
Certain stock imagery © Thinkstock.

Printed in the United States of America

ISBN: 978-1-4525-6196-7 (sc)
ISBN: 978-1-4525-6195-0 (e)
ISBN: 978-1-4525-6197-4 (hc)

Library of Congress Control Number: 2012923418

Balboa Press rev. date: 12/12/2012

Stories of
Inspire-ation,
Love,
and Life

Choose to inspire.

TABLE OF CONTENTS

Dedication:

I dedicate this to my dad, Don (1930-2010), who came back into my life in spirit to heal my heart. And to my beautiful Elia, for her love and eternal acceptance of me for who I am.

When we get rid of
the whys, we then
become the wise.

Love,
Emmanuel

MY LADY
OF THE MORNING

For many years, I wanted to make a difference in someone's life, until one day I realized I already had. I realized that I was a teacher, medium, and healer. I was a magical storyteller with healing words to share.

May these stories inspire and transform you in amazing and abundant ways. *I will always love you.* No matter what.

Emmanuel

*I*t's funny how my entire life I have helped people find their inspiration, their happy thought. Today, I finally found mine: me!

Let's start with today and the lady at the bus stop. My wife, Elia, needed a specific surgery, so after researching, we found the right doctor. Well, he happened to be in Arizona. We happened to be living in Boston at the time, so that would mean traveling. No worries; we didn't mind traveling. So off we went to Arizona, to this land of heat and dry air. We loved it, but we wouldn't get much time to enjoy it, because Elia was having surgery in two days and the rest of the two weeks there would be spent in the hospital. That meant I would be spending a lot of time walking to and fro alone. For me, I am never alone, as my children always told me. I talked to everyone and could probably sell coal to the devil if need be, since I loved to share so much—not that I believe in the devil, mind you. I don't. But what I do believe in is the power of love and sharing that.

So my lovely wife had her surgery, and all was going well. She was healing beautifully. One morning on my way to the hospital, while passing people and greeting them with a cheer–filled, "Good morning," I saw this old lady sitting at the bus stop.

I thought she was priceless. She reminded me of my grandmother, a bit miserable and aged from life, but I knew she looked older than she actually was. In my opinion, it was the way she felt life was treating her that made her look the way she did. Personally, I thought that she was beautiful, so as I describe her, don't misunderstand how I thought she looked. Again, I saw her as beautiful, as she was.

Now the lovely lady sat on this bench like a very sad puddle. You could say she projected misery. It was as if she was saying, "Don't talk to me." I just wanted to hug her, but trust me, I knew better because, like I said, she reminded me of my grandmother, and hugging was the last thing on my grandmother's mind. Well, she was puffing on a cigarette, with only a couple of teeth left in her mouth. She had on these dingy blue pants and shirt and had this big floppy denim hat on her head. She had shaggy, shoulder-length gray hair popping out around the bottom of the hat. She was sitting the way you would if you wanted no one to notice you. You know the way: head turned away, hat covering most of the face so you didn't have to make eye contact. However, she had no idea who was coming up the street, and that was me.

I am always a man on a mission, and my mission is everywhere. I love making eye contact with everyone I meet. I love hugs and chatter. I like to get under your skin in the most loving way with fun, laughter, and love in my heart. I love to find a way to help you see the light that's in you and remember mine too, all wrapped up into one nice package.

Well, she noticed me coming a split second before I got to her, and that was it. I was right, and I knew it as she turned her head the opposite direction as if to say, "I am not here. Leave me alone." She gave out a puff of smoke, and I said to her as cheerfully as possible, "Good morning." I wanted to laugh right out loud as she just looked at me—really, just looked. She gave me that mean stare that said, "Don't bother talking to me. I am *soooo* not interested." You know the look that says, "Why are you talking to me? Hello! Is there a sign on my head that says I want to talk to you? Go away. I don't know you, and I don't want to. It's morning. I am miserable.

Leave me alone."

Oh my land, such enticing words of a good morning to me. Need I say I am being sarcastic? I smiled and said to her, "Have a nice day." It was as if I had toilet paper hanging from the back of my pants, based on the stare she was giving me. I bet she wouldn't have said a word to me if you had paid her. No worries to me as I chuckled to myself and was off to the hospital to see my lovely Elia.

It felt good to have greeted her. I thought about how I always wished my grandmother had taken the time to get to know me in life. I loved her, but in life, she made it clear to me with her words: "Of all of the grandchildren, I never liked you." I always thought that it didn't matter, as one day I told that to my grandmother and then added, "Because I have always loved you, Grandma. Always."

When the next morning arrived, I was up bright and early. It must have been all of that meditating, which I highly recommend; however, I was off and walking my morning trek to the hospital.

How wonderful it was to be greeting people along the way, giving them a morning blessing. Most would answer back, while others were plugged into their own electrical worlds, hoping you wouldn't try to get in. *They don't know me. . . . Could it be? Is that my little old lady sitting at the bus stop again?* I thought. I would just have to say good morning and wish her a great day. Off I was, and way down ahead of me, there she was. I could see her dull, faded clothing, the hat again, and yes, there she was in all her beautiful glory.

As I neared, she looked my way, and I thought that I was going to laugh right out loud. I told myself, "Don't you dare," because she turned her body around so fast to avoid me. Well, if you've ever seen me, then you know that there is no avoiding me unless you run, and sometimes that doesn't even help because I might run after you.

I said, "Hello, good morning," and I leaned so she could see I was looking at her. Again, I just wanted to laugh because when she looked—and I mean *looked*—at me, she gave me the world-famous "look." We've all had that look given to us—the one that says, "Go away. You're bothering me, and I don't want to talk to you, so why, oh why, are you talking to me?"

I chuckled to myself and said to her, "It's going to be another beautiful day," with an added, "Have a great day," I was off again to the hospital to see my lovely wife.

Could my day get any brighter? The thought of that sweet lady stayed with me, and that happy smile crept across my face every time I thought of her throughout the day. It also made me reminisce about how much I always loved my grandmother. She was hard because of the time she lived in and the choices she believed she had to make. Unfortunately for my grandmother, she didn't ever feel that she actually had her own choice.

We all have a choice. When it comes to simple things like a smile, we all have a choice. But then again, we have a choice, period, no matter what the case. I love my choices, and I love sharing the love I know I have inside.

The next day was another perfect day for me in the land of Arizona. I had been using this new meditation and was now meditating for at least an hour a day: thirty minutes of meditation for connecting and maintaining a connection and then thirty minutes that I may have a blessed and peaceful rest. Yep, that's my meditating. It was working; I used to sleep till noon, but now I was waking up between five thirty and six thirty in the morning, which was truly a new one for me. The best part was that I was, and am, still waking up rested for a full day of me.

Up and down the streets of Arizona I was walking, taking pictures along the path of the state's beauty. The flowers and all of their colors gave me the sense of walking amid a warm and soothing rainbow. The birds were chirping and singing their songs to me, talking to me along the path, and then I rounded my favorite corner to see my favorite lady sitting there while waiting for the bus again.

This was getting so fun and familiar, touching someone who wanted to let everyone on the planet think she wanted to be left alone. But I had been in that space of aloneness and knew better. I knew in my heart that she was just afraid. She didn't think that she had a choice—like my grandmother—and I could tell that she wished she could be freer like me. But because she was older and set in her ways, she wasn't going to change. Life had been mean, and that was that. Why change in a world that doesn't care?

Guess what? If you are reading this, I care. I care that you may feel lonely and sad. I have been there when no one wanted to talk to me, and that felt like the worst thing in the world. In high school, I felt like a leper because I wasn't like the others; I wouldn't follow the crowd. Yes, life was hard on me, but I said no to the crap in life and washed it off. I chose to make the choice to believe in me. I am believable to believe in; I am awesome. I love to love and you are loved. I was going to do my best to give a bit of love out each and every day, even when no one seemed to want it, because deep inside, I knew and know, all everyone wants to feel love. Deep inside, I know you want to feel love, and I love you.

I smiled as I looked up and saw my favorite lady again sitting there smoking and waiting for the bus. *Bless her*, I thought, *I can say good morning again. Maybe I'll get a smile back today.*

"Good morning," I said as she again tried her best to avoid me. Each time I kept thinking, *Grandma, I know you wanted my love. You just were afraid to show that you cared.* A smile and a "have a great day" were given her way. I was glowing, and I mean glowing. My Elia was feeling good, and I was resting. I was happy to see my new morning friend. Whether she wanted to see me or not, she was there and so was I.

I was already familiar with her turning and avoiding me. I was just there to give her the message; after all, I was just a messenger delivering morning cheer. Don't you feel that if you start out on a happy note, your day goes so much better? I do. I love giving it out in the morning— happy thoughts, that is. Just to let you know, she hadn't made a sound to me yet, but I kept thinking I had a few more days. and if she's there in the morning, I will keep smiling and do my best to help her along life's journey. She gave me the look again with eyebrows all crinkled up. I smiled, told her to have a nice day, and walked on.

I arrived at the hospital and told my wife about my lady of the morning. "You know what," I told her. "I am going to stop and chat with her if she's there in the morning, because every day she's in the same spot, same place. Same, same, same, every day."

My day went well, and when I thought of my lady of the morning, I just continued to think of my grandmother and smiled. I always wished I could have had my grandmother as mine, as she never was.

The next morning came, and I thought, *Man, I am thirty minutes late. I hope she's there, but if she's on a schedule, I have missed her.* I thought to myself I am not going to worry about it. If it was meant to be, it was meant to be and that was that. I was just going to trust. I greeted my usual passersby, tripped at my usual spot on the sidewalk path, rounded the corner, and looked up to see if my lady of the morning was there. My heart skipped a beat, as she was there sitting, but that morning was different.

She was sitting there, yes, but with her back to the street. Yes, she was still avoiding me, but today she had no floppy hat. She was uncovered. Her beautiful hair was straight and lovely. Nothing fussy, ya know? It was just washed, parted in the middle, and brushed straight. *How beautiful,* I thought. Her head was down as I said, "Good morning."

She looked up today without that grimace on her face. She just looked up! No, she hadn't made a sound, but I was already moved. She was still there, and there was no grim look looking back at me. I had decided to strike up a conversation no matter what, and wow, she was finally looking at me.

So, I told her, "Ya know what? I am sure gonna miss you when I no longer see you here in the morning." I told her that my Elia was in the hospital and that I would have to buy a new suitcase because of airport damage. And then I looked at her and said, "So, are you off to work?"

In a very pleasant tone, she answered, "No."

Yes, I thought, *a connection. You got her to talk.* I said to her, "Oh, just off for a ride, huh?" Then I smiled and added, "Well, I was told the mall is up the street there a bit."

She said, "Yeah, the Camel Back Mall. It's a nice mall."

I just wanted to cry, as we were now actually talking. "So, it's not far?" I asked fully knowing already that the mall was about two miles up.

She said, "No, it's not far."

I smiled and said, "Well, I am only going have maybe one more day to chat with you before I go back to my home, as I am from the east." She nodded her head. I stepped forward and reached out my hand to shake hers. "It was nice to have met you and chatted with you," I said.

She reached out and touched my hand and gave me the handshake back. I felt awesome. It was a moment of love to remember—a touchdown of the heart and soul. I had finally made it past the goal line. Score, as a golden star was posted on the wall of glory in the universe. How beautiful, as she barely looked at me with this shy smile, and then I saw her eyes. Those eyes were one of the most beautiful sights ever. I could see my grandmother's eyes in hers. They were an amazing icy blue—stunning.

I looked at her and said, "You have the most beautiful blue eyes."

She beamed. What a moment I shared with this stranger on the streets of Arizona. I am sure she didn't set out each day to see me, but I am glad our paths crossed. I was touched by her love, and my love. I saw it in her eyes. I cried that day. And I cried as I wrote this. It doesn't take much to smile to someone; it doesn't take much to share a hello with a stranger each day. It doesn't take much of an effort to hold a door for someone. Really. Try it and see how you feel when you take the moment to freely send some love to a stranger.

To be totally free, one must free themselves from the opinions of others.

Love,
Emmanuel

INSPIRATION

*O*MG. I sit here crying as I am listening to the Canadian Tenors. I must tell you why.

It has been so many years that I can't even tell you how many years have passed. I was so used to abuse as a child. Back then, it was called "spare the rod, spoil the child." My family's preacher would preach this tune. I remember being taken out on the church steps and having my bottom beat so that I would go back inside to sit still. Now how that makes sense, I will never know. I have always had to be my own source of inspiration.

For most of my life I was battered and knocked down till I grew big enough to stop the abuse and then when physical abuse couldn't happen, my family group would mentally abuse. I rose above it. I rose above it all. So whenever you think you can't people, I am here to tell you *yes you can!*

Be there for you. Lift yourself up.

Fill yourself so full of love that you are blinding to even yourself. If you could feel the love I fully feel for all of you... you would just burst as I love me and can share this amazing love I know as Emmanuel. If you can, listen to Canadian Tenor's song "Always There," think of *you*, and know that somewhere out there in this universe, I love you.

It was many years ago, when my babies were very small, I wanted to do something special. I didn't have a lot of money, but I did have an abundance of love. So I took a few dollars for an idea I had and then went to the bathroom. Wow, so what am I going to do with the money in the bathroom, right? I was actually going to just put it in my pocket, as I needed the bathroom mirror. Had you for a moment, right? Well, get ready, because I took out some makeup I had and did my eyes all up and then covered my face and lips and before you knew it, I had a lovely mime's face painted on me. I had a mission that day, and that was to bring cheer to as many as my idea would allow.

So I got in my car and off I was to the mall, waving to the masses on the way. I loved every time someone would look, as I would just smile and wave. What joy I felt when I reached the mall thirty-five minutes later. Then it was time to find a florist to finish my plan. I found the florist and bought the biggest bouquet I could and I was ready.

I started looking for the saddest people—you know, the ones not strong enough to stand on their own just yet. And every time I saw a sad person I would walk right up to them, hand them a flower, and smile. I must say this went on for some time till all the flowers were gone. I never knew how many people I had touched that day; I only know that it had touched me deeply. I cried with this amazing joy all the way home. My heart was full, and my cup was running over. I couldn't wait to get home and share.

I told my wife what I had done, and she couldn't believe I had spent money on flowers just to give them away. But isn't that what we do anyhow? Don't we all buy flowers for the ones we love, and then that's that? I smiled knowing I had touched many people that day. I smiled knowing still, that somewhere out there in this world, there are people who will never forget the day this painted mime walked up to them in their moments of sadness and handed them beauty. I will never forget—never.

See the inspiration, ... feel the inspiration, ... and then just be the inspiration.

Fore *I* am inspiration!

Life is just a game.
You win when you
remember who you are.

Love,
Emmanuel

A LITTLE BOY'S LOVE

I have always taught my children—all six of them—to be loving and kind. Whether or not they are as adults is always their choice; however, I will never forget many years ago a touching moment with my oldest.

My children were always watching me make things constantly and then give them away. I'd always had a talent when it came to creating something out of nothing and then giving it to someone to enrich their life. That was just what I felt life should be. I knew that the universe watched over me and that I would always have enough. Every time my wife thought that we might not have something to eat, I would tell her, "Don't worry. We will always have enough." And we always did.

I was always making wooden toys for the children, as my father had a sawmill and whenever I could, I would go to the sawmill and take a board to use for a gift for someone. I would plane it, sand it, cut it, paint it, and then give it away. For years I made Christmas ornaments for my children's classes—hundreds of wooden ornaments. My children were quite familiar with me doing this for others.

One day my son did something quite spectacular. A tragedy happened that day—the bombing of the Alfred P. Murrah Federal Building in Oklahoma City. At my children's school, they watched as the people of Oklahoma City went through a bombing. My heart went out to the people at that time as many people's hearts went out to people that day. After hearing about the tragedy, my son Caleb started thinking about something. He started wondering what he could do for the people of Oklahoma. It was a what-would-Daddy-do moment." Would you believe that in his elementary school my son decided to take up a collection all on his own, just as he had watched his father do for many years. I was always doing my best to help others along life's path. I knew tragedy and knew there was life beyond it. For a few days he walked around his elementary school collecting until one day he brought me a surprise.

I had been working all day in my workshop. At the time I was drinking tea and zoning in my peaceful place. I loved my workshop, as it was so magical. I had forgotten that the bus was probably there, and all of a sudden my beautiful son appeared and said, "Hi, Daddy." Those were magical words for me because all I had ever dreamed about was being a dad, and there was my cutie staring at me and greeting me with his abundance of love. "How was your day?" he asked me.

I told him that Daddy's day went so well that he had forgotten about time and I was sorry that I didn't meet him at the bus stop. He told me that was okay. I asked him how his day was, and he said to me, "Oh, pretty good. Here, " he said "I have something for you. I brought you home a Blow Pop."

I said to him, "Where did you get that?"

He said, "Oh, I did a nice thing in school today, so my teacher gave it to me."

I told him that was nice and to go on inside and put away his school stuff, do his chores, and get ready for dinner. I told him I would be right in.

It took me a bit of time, as sometimes I do get lost in thought about what I am working on, but as time passed I started thinking, *I am going to have to ask him what the good deed was that his teacher treated him for.* Next thing you know, I had forgot about time again, and he was out of the house and behind me once again. "Hi, Daddy," he said. What magical words for me to hear once again.

I stopped working and said to him, "By the way, what good thing did you do that the teacher gave you a treat?"

He said to me, "Well, remember the Oklahoma City bombing the other day?"

I said, "Yes."

He said, "Well, I went through the school and collected over three hundred dollars to donate to the people and the families who were hurt by the bombing. Do you think this will help them?"

So priceless that this little man of mine felt such compassion for the people of Oklahoma. I was so proud just to know this little man. I was so proud that I could call him my son. He had always made me proud since the moment he had been born, and now he was eight going on ninety-eight—what a man.

By this moment tears were pouring down my face as my little boy, all on his own, had done something so amazing as raise money to help others in need. What a special young man. We sent the money on and never heard back, but I can tell you this: that never meant a thing to my little man. He was just so proud that he could do something.

That was many years ago, and today my little boy is now a grown man—a lawyer in a few states and still as awesome as ever. In life sometimes while you're not looking, others are, and they are being guided by the bright light that is you. So remember, even when you think they are not watching, they truly are.

Precious Times to Last

Son, slow down, don't grow up fast
I want these precious times to last.
Like read a book, or fix my car
How 'bout a drink, or is it far?
I'm yucky, Daddy, the sink's too high
Let's brush our teeth, just let me try.
I want a cup, I'm thirsty now
Where's are all my toys? Hey, that's a cow.
Or this is mine, and that is too
For all the times I spend with you …
So … Son, slow down; don't grow up fast
I need these precious times to last.

Love,

Emmanuel

BEING YOURSELF

Sometimes the greatest way to inspire someone is to just be who you are. No wait; the best way to inspire is to always be yourself. At times being who you are can seem to be a difficult thing, but when you live by the motto "what you think of me is none of my business," the rest is just a breeze.

My children have always said to me, "Padre, you are eccentric." For a time, I just didn't get it. Each time I would do something they would say it again. I would paint the trim in my house gold, and they would say you are so eccentric. I would wear my tuxedo with my red sneakers, and they would say the same thing. I was always saying, "I don't get it, as I am just being who I am."

My children would always laugh and say, "Padre, not very many think and act the way you do."

I would still say to them, "Well, I don't get it, because I think all should be free to be who they are and just be that way."

So, was it always that way? Hmm… the answer would be yes. I remember my life growing up in my home where I was called a freak—not a guy or a girl, queer, fag, weirdo. My parents would say that I wasn't like the rest of their children. "You're just different from the rest," my family would all say. I didn't care for the names, but for me, I was perfect and special the way I was. I liked short shorts when long shorts were in and straight leg jeans when bells were in. Heck, if I had my way, I would never get dressed, but people are so not ready for that. Right? So what's the deal? I say, just don't care what others think, because that is none of your business. Be free to be who you are. Yes, I have been publicly laughed at and made fun of, and I cared, because at that time I cared what others thought. But, hey, I wanted to be me. I wanted to be free from the confines of what others thought, so I started living with the belief what others think of you is none of your business. You know what happened? I became so much happier.

I started wearing my wraps everywhere I went. People, I am sure, were looking, but I wasn't. I was no longer looking for their reaction. I was only looking where I was going. I can remember my first marriage so many years ago. I walked out of the bathroom one day with my toenails painted gold and wearing a ripped and tie-dyed T-shirt with a wrap (ankle-length, of course) tied around my waist. I was ready to go to the store with my wife and children. I will never forget her words: "Aren't you going to change?"

The words in my head were, "Why yes, Dear, I have already changed a lot. I have actually grown accustomed to me, and me likes this." However, that would have caused a large argument; me being myself wasn't working for her. My, I need to be me was not what she needed. Funny how when you first marry, the things that make you unique are awesome and so attractive, but if you don't conform to what someone's friends say, you begin to become the outcast.

For me I had been the outcast since I was born. No new news to me. I felt that I was not an outcast but an *in*cast and that being me would make a great difference—well, at least for me. I was growing quite accustomed to being me. I had always felt special, you know? I totally felt that sparkle inside and wanted to let it out.

Yes, there was that time when I had the crap beat out of me for being who I was and that totally didn't make sense to me. So when one of my parents told me I was no more special than any other but then treated me like the odd one of the bunch, I knew they knew but just weren't sure how to love someone so different from their norm.

No worries. I grew up, grew away, and became as special as I wanted to be, because if you feel it and can't be it, you will just die somehow of sadness. I always had this vast need to be me no matter what was beat out of me. What was truly me could not be beaten out. My soul glimmered so bright that it was blinding, and blinding I liked. One day a divorce came my way, and the true love of my life finally came into my view, the one I now call Elia, my wife. She walked into my world loving every moment about me—what an angel. She loved my sparkle from the get-go and followed suit. She told me later that I was her inspiration to finally freely be who she always wanted to be: free.

Awesome.

She learned these words fast: what you think about me is none of my business. And she decided to ride the wave. I would wear my gold nails and my pearls and never hear a complaint. I would put on my wraps and hear, "Oh, that's beautiful." I would wear sparkles on my eyes and skin everywhere and she would just ask for some so she could sparkle too. I loved it. Then one day she learned the fullness of the sparkles.

One day a friend of ours came over for dinner, and I had forgotten to put my sparkles on. She noticed, so I went and put them on. She was thrilled and said to me, "It just wasn't you without that sparkle—that Emmanuel sparkle."

Then one day she texted me and said, "You'll never guess what happened. I took out my phone to make a call, and these sparkles fell right on my hand. I don't even know where they came from, but I thought, *Hey, they are Emmanuel's sparkle!*" She remembered how much she loved me and how much I loved her. Just a sparkle, but it also sparked a memory of a beautiful moment.

I remember preaching a spiritual talk one day and mentioning to someone, "Could you imagine if you could track how many lives you touch a day and how that would make you feel?" I can tell you that I would feel awesome—really, really awesome. I thought about it and said to my Elia, "If I could gather up all the people who have sparkles on them because of the hugs or handshakes or touches I give out every day,

I would have football fields of people." Now how cool of a thought is that, right? So with that said, I was quite moved by my realization.

Every morning I do my best to give everyone I see a smile, so if I could monitor the smiles that now carry on because of me, how many more sparkles would that be? More football fields of people appeared in my mind. Then I thought about all of the people I tell to have a good day or have a nice day or an awesome day or great day. How many more people would be in that football field touched by me? I thought about all of the people I am polite to just because it's a nice and right thing to do. I find that no matter how much people tried to beat that out of me the I-gotta-be-me mentality stayed. I am glad, because I love knowing that every moment I touch someone with love, they touch someone with love, and that is the ripple in my pond.

This is just me being *me!* Now just be you.

What if life was just a test to see
how far your love could go?
Would you pass?

Love,

Emmanuel

FALLING IN
LOVE TO SPARKLE

So what's it like to fall in love? I mean really fall in love. I love that song "Falling in Love Again." So sweet aah... I mean falling in love with yourself. It's like finding a part of you everywhere you go. It's seeing you in all things, everywhere. It's leaving a trail of you every moment of every day. It's like always finding sunshine in a dark room just because you're there.

I remember when I first started wearing sparkles. What a fun day it was for me. But more fun was last week, or was it just a few weeks ago? Hmm ... anyhow, before I digress too far, let's start in a place call Rhinebeck, NY. It was a week with James Van Praagh.

Well, being me, I got up, took a shower, dressed, and put on sparkles. You know what I mean, right? Sparkles—those little tiny things, that mean I am stuck to you all day and then some. Each day I would sparkle, each day I would hug the multitudes, and each day all would travel the day with sparkles. By the end of the day, you could see how many had been hugged by me in the room. It is fun, as it always is, to leave a trail of love. I love to see what part of me I can see in you that's me, and then I can remember to get a hug from me from you too. Sometimes the me I'm looking at doesn't quite remember it's me, but I just give me a smile, and usually, I get the hug. The um......... okay... I'll give you a hug. To me that means I helped me to get the me in you to sparkle too—well, the me that's in you. You get that, right? I am in me and I am in you.

Are you too confused? If you are, that's okay. I'm not, but I sure am smiling.

So what does this have to do with falling in love with yourself? Everything. When you can look at someone and see yourself in them, it makes you look forward to seeing them over and over. Are you understanding yet? Come on, you've gotta be getting this by now. I know it—I really do and you do too.

I know that for a week of metaphysical learning I got to know a room full of people, all different yet all the same. All mes (because we are all me and we are all you), just a bit different. It was kind of like I went to a closet and put on all different outfits just so I could see what I looked like different from the usual me. The thing is that I lost a way to keep track of me. So one day I decided I would have to leave a marker, and that would be sparkles. That way, I would always be able to remember me. *What a great idea*, I thought. That way every time I hug me (you) I will remember that I have touched me with love and left a mark, a spark, a sparkle that says to me, "Remember you touched me." So, with that said (and, yes, it's all about *me*), my story begins.

I and my wife were a bit sad about leaving Rhinebeck. I know for me, I fall in love with, well, almost everyone I meet. I guess there are a few of mes who don't care for me yet. I will work on that. So we left the gathering and cried almost all of the way home, and that would be about three hours. I think dehydration was setting in. Just kidding, we had an amazing time. We arrived home and connected to the world so as to keep in touch with the love of so many who had touched us and the lives that we had touched as well.

It would be a short time before we would be off to Arizona. My lovely Elia needed a surgery. She would be staying in the hospital for eight days, and while she was there, I would be walking to and from our motel and the hospital. What an adventure for us.

Our first day was spent getting there and getting ready. The first day was exciting, meeting all of the new people on our adventure. I would be sitting in the waiting room for most of the day, but hey, I was ready. With my sparkles on, I was ready to meet and reach out to greet and be greeted by whoever wanted to come my way. Some would walk my way and just stare, but others would walk by and when I said hello, they would smile and say hi back. That to me is always a success—a connection. But a hug? Now that's another success. That's recognizing love and wanting to have that hug touching back. I love hugs.

Well, without ever knowing it, I was leaving a trail—a trail that symbolized me. I was leaving a trail of sparkles. I have to laugh, because only a few days earlier we were in our home in Boston and a friend was over for dinner. Being a chef, I not only love to cook, but I live to love to cook. With that said, I and Elia had company coming over, so I was cooking and had forgotten to put on sparkles. It was so wonderful when she said to me after arriving, "Hey, Emmanuel, where are your sparkles? You are not you without your sparkles." Sounds familiar? I know; it happens everywhere I go. Priceless.

I left the room and put on my sparkles. I was so thankful for the reminder, as it was becoming a common thing among friends—get your sparkles on. I was grateful for the reminder. While we were in Arizona, she sent us a text message saying that she picked up her glass and when she did she saw sparkles on her hand and knew it was me. It brought tears to my eyes knowing the reminder of me was a blessing of love and light to her. A couple of tiny sparkles were gleaming light on her hand, and she knew the sparkles were from me.

So as it goes, I was in the waiting room leaving a few sparkles on the furniture (not intentionally, of course), and as I walked, a few would occasionally fall off. Little did I know at the time that everywhere I went I was leaving reminders of me and my love for all. Funny; as I write this, sparkles are on my computer reminding me to give that light to me and to you everywhere I go.

The first day in Arizona was awesome meeting people on the floor in the waiting area and meeting Julie in the nurses' area. I had no idea where to go. The doctor had told me to ask the nurse where I could wait for my wife until she was out of surgery. So I asked a nurse and noticed her name was Julie.

Julie was lovely and had an awesome smile. Her energy was so lovely, that I felt her loving heart immediately. I told her my dilemma, and she showed me the way. I smiled, as it was the way to the waiting room. I went there with a smile, thinking how funny Julie was in her comment to me. "Yes," she said. "I know where you can wait, and that's over there in the waiting room."

I took no offense. I just smiled and said, "Oh I just didn't know."

"Oh that's okay," she said with a sweet smile. And we both shared a lovely laugh and bond. I was ever so grateful for Julie's sweetness. She saw how much a mess I was, with the love of life my being somewhere I didn't know. She gave me comfort and that's all I needed. Thanks Julie.

I waited for Elia to be brought to her room so that I could be with her. I had left sparkles in another waiting room. I would be meeting more of the staff that I and Elia would be falling in love with. We would be meeting new people every day, and soon people would be wearing sparkles that they didn't know they were wearing. Soon I would be touching more than I knew. Soon my heart would be touched in ways like it had never been before. Each day at the hospital I would come just as me—clothed and sparkled.

I would meet with my beloved Elia, and there would be a new set of nurses and aides everyday, finding new sparks of love forming with them all. We would all talk of life and love, and love and life. We would share stories with them and hear stories back; all the while, our hearts were falling in love with them. I would help lift Elia's spirit and help lift others too. While I wasn't there, Elia would be sharing and when I would get there, I would begin telling true stories of our life and loves and paths that life had taken us. We met other patients; all the while, we felt we were just sharing.

One day someone asked why I wore sparkles, and I explained, to match my personality and share a bit of me with them. I wear sparkles because that's how my soul feels inside. My soul sparkles with the gold and that's how I feel and I have to get it out. When I put them on, I just feel so me. I said I love to hug, and when I hug, a bit of me comes off on you. They liked that and left with a smile. I liked it too, as sparkling was how I felt inside—all aglow. Elia also liked it when I wore sparkles, so that was that.

We were able to meet more patients and share with them stories of healing. I loved telling stories, as it was always a way to connect with someone who needed to take their mind off of sadness and worries and problems of the day. It was always a way to help others hear and let go of their stress. Funny, but I had never thought about how I helped heal people. I had always laid healing hands on people but had never thought that my words healed until I started hearing people thank me for my words as they were so healing. They would say, "You have no idea how healing your words are and were to me." That took me by surprise, as I was never thinking about my words being healing.

I had always felt that sharing my words was loving, and I loved to share love. I know that we are all teachers and all students. That day I was the student in awe, but tears came because I was in awe of me. Our sweet, cheerful Nurse Lisa taught me that I was always a bundle of light and joy. I would give her thanks and say, "Lisa, you are that special too." She also liked my sparkles.

Well, every day on the way to the hospital I would greet and meet new people. I would meet them walking. I would meet them at the grocery store. I would meet them at the bookstore. Funny thing: I walked into the bookstore one day, and the store was quiet and dim, but before you knew it, daylight seemed to be pouring in from everywhere.

The guys behind the counter had been withdrawn with their heads lowered a bit. When I walked in, they were not saying much until I finally walked up to the counter and told them about my wife in the hospital and the love we share and how much fun these stores are. Our conversation took off in an amazing adventure of light, as they enjoyed someone coming in who was there to have fun in life and not fear. I told them I loved life and loved to shine my light everywhere, and before I left, we all knew each other by our first names and were laughing for all to wonder about.

No matter where you go in life, if you glow, you just glow no matter how much light is there, because you know what I am? I am a beacon of light, and I love to shine, so shine in that store I did. I also left a bit of sparkle behind when I shook their hands good-bye. Sometimes people forget with their judgments that we all have hearts and we all feel. Sometimes it's just nice to let others know you have a heart that cares. But no matter, I was there just being me and not thinking about what I had left behind except hopefully a smile and a good memory or two.

Well, it was almost the end of the week, and I and Elia were feeling a bit sad that we would soon be leaving. We had one more day before we were to leave. I was walking in the hospital that morning when all of a sudden I noticed some sparkles on the sidewalk. I had to laugh, as I noticed that they were my sparkles. That morning I had noticed that the hotel couch had a few sparkles on it, and I smiled thinking, *I bet a few years from now I will still have a sparkle or two left behind in this hotel room.*

As I kept walking, now on my path to the hospital, I would see a few sparkles here and there along the way. It made me smile. I arrived at the hospital and noticed some sparkles in Elia's room. I had noticed that some of the people I had hugged in the hospital had a few sparkles on them still, and as I and Elia walked the circle of the hospital floor, I had to laugh as I saw a few sparkles in the carpet of the hospital rug. I showed Elia, and we just had to smile as I seemed to leave a part of me everywhere I went.

Pretty soon Friday came, and we were so filled with tears to see the day arrive. I was still wearing my sparkles. Now I was trying my best to keep a straight face so as not to cry with sparkles. We just wanted to leave with a smile. Then this beautiful woman walked in the room and said to Elia, "Ya know what? I know you won't mind if I do this," and she took her hands, held my face, and rubbed my face all over hers. And then she said, "I just wanted some of that sparkle too."

I was honored. I had touched a few, and the few had touched me. Elia had touched them too, and for that we knew, we would be blessed forever.

We took some pictures, said our good-byes, and walked down to say good-bye to another patient. It was so sad leaving, but when a baby bird has wings, she must fly. So it was out of the nest for us and soon time to fly. We walked back out of the room and said good-bye, startling one of our favorite people. We didn't mean to; it just happened. She said, "You're back," with such joy. Her eyes were filled with that teary stuff—you know, that stuff that leaks out of your eyes when your heart has been touched and you don't want to say anything or acknowledge that you have been crying. You know we've all done it.

Elia and I were touched and knew we were so blessed to have been able to spend eight days with some of the most amazing and loving people in the world. We loved them. I told myself I wouldn't cry, because Elia warned me that if I cried, she knew that she would cry too. I was biting my lip to hold back the ocean-sized waterfall. I knew if the dam broke, a flood was coming. We said good-bye again and walked with our cheerful selves to the elevator. The doors closed, and the ocean broke. I couldn't hold the tears back any longer, as I had done what I always do and had fallen in love with all of them.

Elia and I stood there in the elevator crying tears of how wonderful it had been to get to know all of these wonderful loving beings. After all, they had taken the best of care of the one I love, my Elia. All of a sudden the tears were flowing, and the door opened and there standing in front of us was Julie, the nurse who had greeted me when I came in the *very first day*. Julie was there to greet me, and now Julie was there to send us off. More tears would fall as we hugged and watched now two of our friends, both Julies, our housekeeper and our nurse, standing behind the door as it closed.

We tried to be so strong and in the end only got caught in the act of showing how much we really cared. We cried halfway back to the motel and then fell silent for a few moments till I looked over and saw some of my sparkles on Elia. There was some on her face and a few in her hair. Then I thought about how we had hugged as many as we could before we left. How many had sparkles on them? How many lives had Elia and I touched with love while we were there?

We got back to our room at the motel, and Elia said, "Look! There are sparkles on the couch from you".

I smiled and said, "Baby, I have left them everywhere. You know what I think? Every time one of the nurses sees a sparkle, she is going to remember us, and that will be a happy thought. Matter of fact, won't it be great if they are walking around the circle on the floor one day and see a sparkle or two? It will give whomever a nice memory and smile remembering us."

Who knows, maybe one day you, the reader, will be walking along a pathway and see some sparkles glistening in the sun. Guess what, they might just be me left behind. Maybe you will be waiting in a hospital waiting room and see some sparkles there, and you will think, *Could that be Emmanuel?* Who knows, you might even be staying in a hotel/motel one day and find sparkles on the furniture. If you do, my advice is sit where they are. Let them then be carried off by you to then share with someone else and be left by you. I like to think that a sparkle was my calling card left behind for you to see—that I was there just waiting for you to find that sparkle that was part of me.

"Life is just a lesson
in the sea of Love"

Love,
Emmanuel

BEING WHERE
YOU NEED TO BE

*A*s it happened, our morning was awesome. I never eat breakfast, but I wanted to be up with Elia. We were staying at a hotel at the moment, so I would go downstairs with her and at least have coffee. I hurried and finished up with my shower, got dressed up in my ripped T-shirt and sarong (or what I call a wrap), covered my face and body with sparkles, and was ready for the day. I really wanted to wear my coveralls so I could walk downtown with Elia and have room for my wallet and loose money, but I just kept leaning toward the wrap.

"Want me to wear the bibs today?" I asked Elia.

She said, "No, why don't you wear your wrap today?" So wrap it was.

I was having a pain that I was unfamiliar with. So I felt that someone who was in spirit was sending me messages to let me know they wanted to communicate. That was one way I would be able to identify them. I was given a few more messages and said to the soul who wanted to connect, "If this is a message and this pain belonged to you, I need it to be removed now so I know it's proof of you." Immediately, the pain went away, so I knew it was a message of who this spirit was.

I got a few more messages when I spoke to the spirit again. "I want proof—name, how you died, birth date, or death date time." I wanted more details and nothing more, so I said to the soul, "No connection till there is more proof given."

Elia and I walked downstairs to breakfast. Elia found the breakfast bar to be filled with all of her morning delights. Not me, though, as the only thing that I wanted was coffee, and the pot was empty. I saw the kitchen attendant fixing a batch of pancakes and told him as gently as possible, good morning and that I didn't want him to rush, but I wanted him to know that the coffee pot was empty and there were a few people pacing near the coffee pot. He was such a cute, chubby little man.

He smiled at me and said, "Oh yes, I will get to it, sir."

I smiled and told him no worries. I waited, and then he took out the empty pot and brought in another one filled with hot coffee. I thanked him, and off he went cleaning the tables. *What a sweet man*, I thought. I kept hoping he was compensated with a full day's pay for his work and not part of a slave trade, as I noticed the cleaning crew and smaller jobs of the hotel were held by a certain group of people.

I asked the universe to bless them all and I walked on drinking my coffee. Unfortunately, I know that slave trades exist in our beautiful land we call America—home of the free and the brave. So I sat drinking my coffee with Elia, praying for the beautiful workers as she ate her breakfast and sending out blessings to all in the motel.

When we were finished, we left the dining area and went back to our room to freshen up. I couldn't wait to take a walk down town to the Old Town Scottsdale, Arizona. Some of the older buildings of yesteryear were still there. *How wonderful*, I thought. I was hoping that we might be able to find a nice necklace and earrings for Elia to remember the trip by. I had my constant memories of her and how much I loved her, and I needed nothing less or more than her.

We were expecting a guest that day, and Elia was concerned we might miss our soul sister Butterfly. I told Elia to just give Butterfly a call and see if she knew when she would be stopping by. Elia gave her a call and couldn't get through, so she texted her. I kept telling Elia not to worry; Butterfly would call us, and we wouldn't miss her. Elia and I had never before had someone as caring as Butterfly in our lives, so we kind of adopted her as our sister.

With that said, we were off and traveling on our merry way, greeting everyone on our path as always. We neared the old town and could see the older style buildings but noticed we were apparently early. No stores were open. Then we saw it—down the way a bit there was a young man looking at postcards on the street, and we knew something must be open. As we got near, we could see it was a small jewelry store, and they had the most lovely pair of handmade earrings ever. I knew they would be perfect for my Elia. They were hummingbirds made of turquoise. I loved hummingbirds, as they were one of my Native American totems. They were also a reminder to me that my dad was always nearby. It's always a nice reminder to remember my joy. *Perfect*, I thought, *perfect.* Next I would have to find a bracelet to match, and we would be off.

All of a sudden, Elia received a text and it's our Butterfly. She was five minutes away from our hotel. Yikes! As we were about ten to fifteen minutes away, and that was walking distance. Elia called and texted her but didn't get a response. We started walking back to the hotel, but I wouldn't let Elia rush, as she had just gotten out of the hospital from having major surgery and was needing to relax and not rush. I told her we wouldn't miss our Butterfly, as I knew she loved us as we loved her, so not to worry.

As we were walking, I told Elia to try to call her again, thinking maybe she'd get through. Sure enough, she did. Within minutes, our Butterfly was flying our way to pick us up. The walk was lovely and refreshing to us. It was eighty-six degrees and morning, but we didn't mind. We were from the northeast where it's usually colder, so defrosting our bones felt good.

There she was in all of her glory, waving her hand and motioning us to where she was going to be able to pull off the road. We hopped in our Butterfly's bright red coupe convertible, and we were off back to the motel. We chatted and shared and chatted and shared, knowing that this would be the last time we would see our butterfly for at least a few months. Butterfly wanted Elia to know she looked absolutely stunning and wanted to let me know that I looked so sexy in my wrap as it reminded her of the love of her life when he was in the land of the living. He was her wrap kind of guy, wearing a wrap outside or inside, just being free to be who he was—her rock of inspiration and her love.

I knew that this was the reason I had chosen to wear this that morning. I felt the connection. This was why I hadn't worn my coveralls that morning. This was why I was being inspired to wear my wrap. I was touched, as I knew who was trying to get a message through to a loved one. I knew this man wanted to get a message through to the woman he loved in life. I was blessed.

I told him that if he wanted me to give a message, he would have to give more proof than an ache and a wrap, but he wouldn't budge. Our butterfly, however, had more to share. She wanted us to know that she wished she could hear some answers that she had about the love of her life who had died, that she wasn't quite ready to let go.

Ah, I felt I understood why he wasn't giving me any more messages. She wasn't yet ready. I looked at Butterfly, touched her hand, and told her I'd had someone visiting me that morning and I know it was her Rock of love. But I told him I wouldn't tell her anything until he gave me more information for proof of his existence of whom he was in life. I told her now I understood why he wouldn't give me anymore information because as she just stated she was not ready yet. I told her that when she was ready she would get the answers she was looking for as I could guarantee that.

Some tears came into her eyes. And I said to her, "I didn't want to wear this outfit this morning, but I felt I needed to, so this is a confirmation to you that your Rock is here and waiting for when you are ready. So when you are, he will come through someone for sure and be here waiting with the message you are seeking, when you are ready."

I would have given anything to have told her what I knew, but it wasn't my place to go where I hadn't been asked to go. I could see that a healing had begun to take place with just the words that I had shared. She could feel and knew that the love she once knew was there with us, waiting in the car with us with a great love and patience for her tender heart. Elia and I felt so blessed to just be in the car with her for the moment and share what we could. I knew we were where we needed to be. We gathered our stuff and got out of the vehicle. We were hugging and kissing each other's cheeks and doing our best not to cry, but it was time to go.

All of a sudden this beautiful young woman from Texas runs across the parking lot saying, "Hi. I hate to bother y'all, but can I get a picture with all of ya?"

We were stunned and thrilled all in one bundle. "Absolutely," we all said together.

As she got closer, the young lady said, "I know it sounds crazy, but you guys are so beautiful. I just wanted to know if I could get a picture with you. You guys look like movie stars, and y'all are just glowin' like bright lights in the parkin' lot."

We smiled and told her that she was not a bother and of course she could get a picture with us, as we would love to have a picture taken with her. Our Butterfly offered to take the shot with us and our joyful Texan together. She was thrilled. This lady just looked at us all and said again, "You just look so beautiful together I ... I wanted a picture of that. You guys really do glow."

"Thank you so much," I said.

She just stood there smiling at us. What a blessing. I am sure we were shining brightly and sparkling now all together. The moment was over, and we hugged and wished our Texan friend a blessed day. She was off with a smile, and so were we.

Emmanuel

Our Butterfly was flying away, and Elia and I were walking up to our room to rest with tears of joy in our eyes. Elia looked at me and said, "Do we really shine that bright, Emmanuel, that people can actually see it?"

I smiled at my true heart's love and said, "But of course, Sweetie. We beam like the sun shining."

We felt so blessed to have been in the right place at the right time. Yes, it was perfect timing to a perfect day being where we perfectly needed to be at that very moment, a passer walked by. Be who you are, and in that, be the best that you can be. Be the beauty that's you.

Love is the best gift you
can give to anyone.

Love,
Emmanuel

THE BIRTHDAY GIRL

I and Elia were walking down the street, just enjoying the sites when all of a sudden, right before us, there were two girls dancing and twirling in the streets. I loved the freedom they had to be dancing in the streets, and it was in broad daylight—beautiful. That was something *I* would usually be doing.

I can remember about fifteen years ago dancing on the streets of Cairo, Egypt. I was with a group of what they said were "Spiritual, free people." I can also remember saying to them, "Then dance with me if you are so free." They looked at me like I was nuts. I remember I was wearing tan jeans and a brilliantly colored tie-dyed shirt. I felt as if I were a living rainbow. I had all my earrings in (at the time, about ten) and was wearing about ten crystals around my neck. I just had to be the me that was in me. I was told by a few in the group that I should never wear clothes that stand out. I remember thinking at the time you can't contain a heart that glows, and mine was shining as a beacon of sunlight. So who was caring that my clothes were neon, right?

So, I said to the group, "Come dance with me." But no one would dance.

They said, "But what if someone is looking?"

I had to laugh as I said to them, "First of all, who cares if someone is watching as I am sure they are; we are, after all in the city. Secondly, if they are watching, then maybe they will learn how to free themselves too."

My heart was sad for all the people who were with me that day, but I wasn't going to let it stop me from being me and dancing freely. I have always felt that when the spirit wants to dance, I let it dance. So I was remembering that the freedom to dance in the open air was something that I was quite familiar with and enjoyed. Funny how I am still in contact with some of the people I was with that day in Egypt, and they still won't dance. But me, I dance even freely–er. Yes, freely'er; my children call it a "Padre-ism." My own unique vocabulary.

So I was smiling now, as I was seeing these two girls dance on the streets. I couldn't resist telling them that I loved their dancing in the streets. Elia told them how lovely it was to see their freedom with such joy. The one girl was just getting into the taxi and the other stopped and said, "What did you say?"

We told her all over again, and she just beamed and said to us, "At what age did you two become so cool?"

Wow! What an honor to hear such words from such a beautiful and young woman with a group of her friends. All of a sudden, one of her friends in the van said, "Hey, Dianna, come on. Let's go."

Dianna yelled back, "Not yet. I'm interviewing these two cool people." So she repeated, "At what age did you two become so cool?"

I said to her, "For the past eight years we have been together, and it has been magical and we have been so cool together." Then I told her, "Well, actually, I think we have been cool most of our lives. At least I knew I had been."

Dianna just smiled and said, "I bet you have been." Then she asked, "So when did you two meet?"

I said, "We met eight years ago and have been inseparable ever since."

"Really?" she said in such a sweet tone. "How many kids do you have?"

We both said in one voice together, "Eight between us."

It was hysterical to hear her squeal as she said, "Oh *my* God! Eight—wow! There are three in my family. Hey, did I tell you it's my birthday?

I am twenty-six today. Isn't that a great age?" She was awesome, as she continued with, "Yeah, I think that twenty-six is like the perfect age."

Yes, twenty-six is an awesome age, I was thinking, *and I have a few children older and around your age.* Elia's children were older than and younger than her.

Dianna was beautiful, and her energy was awesome. One of her friends yelled yet again, "Dianna, come on. We're waiting." All the while, the taxi was sitting on the street waiting for Dianna to join her friends. She was still yelling back, "It's my birthday, and I'm not done interviewing these guys. Come on; someone come and meet these guys. They are complete awesomeness."

Elia and I were touched by her shine and candor. She said to us, "So where did you meet?"

And we both said in sync, "New York."

I had to laugh when she said, "So was New York City the first place you ever had sex?"

We just started laughing and replied back, "Actually, no."

None of us missed a beat. We were enjoying the interview with Dianna as much as she was. We laughed actually saying , "Syracuse fair," before we even thought about what we had said and laughed yet again.

Dianna just smiled and said, "I bet I can guess what made you fall in love with her." And just as fast she added, "And tell me what it was without even thinking. Come on—fast, fast."

I said to her, "My Elia had the most beautiful soul."

Dianna just stood there touching her heart as she gasped, "Awe."

Yes, that's how I feel all the time—awe. Then she gave us a big hug without hesitation. We were touched, but Dianna wasn't done.

"Ya know what?" she said. "I have this uncle—you know, he is a special uncle. Well, he likes boys."

I smiled and said, "Me too, Dianna. I love everyone." I chuckled as she didn't miss a single beat.

She said, "Hey, I do too, and there's nothing wrong with that, right? I just love him the way he is. He's my very special uncle, but it's because he is so special."

I was good with that. I got her message and understood how beautiful her uncle was.

She said, "Well, he was married three times, and the last time was with a man. Guess who gave him the most support?" she said. "Guess." Again, she was on a roll as she said, "That would be my new uncle who's married to my uncle. Isn't that great?"

I smiled and said, "Dianna, that is awesome. Ya know what? I was married to someone else a long time ago, and that was another woman. She wasn't very happy, and I couldn't make her happy either. Then I met my beauty Elia, and she was a man then. And you know what? I have been so happy ever since."

"One day she says to me, 'You do know I am a woman, don't you?' and I said 'But of course. But I married you because of *love* not because of what you were. I married you because I love you.'"

"And now," I told Dianna, "I am married to a woman because my beauty fulfilled her life's dream, and she became the woman that she is today."

She looked at us and said with the most beautiful sigh, "Awe, I just love you two." And then she said, "Ya know what? I have to go." She looked at her friend who had joined her on the street and said, "But aren't you glad you got to meet the two coolest people in the world with me on my birthday?"

With one more hug, she was off, and so were we. Enjoying life to the fullest in the moment on the streets, remembering it was a girl's twenty-sixth birthday wish to talk to a couple she thought was really neat and super cool.

Happy Birthday, Dianna! May all your wishes come true. I do know you blessed us that day with your freedom to share your love and your birthday with us. Love, Emmanuel and Elia.

Peace doesn't need to make
a sound to be heard.

Love,
Emmanuel

OFF TO MEET MOSTAFA

*I*t was our last day of vacation in the Arizona sunshine, and I wanted to buy something special for my Elia. Her beauty is so magical to me that I love marking the day with something special whenever I can. We were off walking the streets to find the traditional part of town. I love the new, but I love the old and the traditional too. Unfortunately, sometimes the traditions get lost in the color of green, the dollar bill.

That day I didn't care. I just wanted to buy her something pretty. We found a lovely store that had those hummingbirds made of turquoise, and they were stunning. I found a bracelet to match, and there you have it—something beautiful for my lovely Elia.

We had to rush back to meet someone, so we cut our trip short but vowed to go back to the town and walk more a bit later. When later came, we found ourselves walking the older streets once again. It reminded me of when I was a child and we used to travel to Oklahoma. My parents bought me my favorite pair of bib overalls there. They were blue-and-white striped and so me. One of my favorite aunts lived and worked in Oklahoma. She was a sweetie and had an accent that just wouldn't quit.

Anyhow, my parents, not having much money, bought us gifts that were usable and practical. Sometimes as a child I wish it could have just been a toy instead, but I know they did what they could, and that was that. I loved my bibs, and as I remember, I wore them babies out. So walking the streets of an old town brought me to nice, fond memories, of a day gone by. I and Elia walked past the store where I had bought her earrings and wished that they had another pair in the window, as one of her hummingbirds had fallen out of her ear while walking and was now lost. My heart was sad for Elia, because I knew she felt the specialness of the gift. I assured her that they were just earrings and that she was what was most special.

"I know," she said, "but I am going to feel sad about it all day."

Until I told her, "Now, Elia, you are special—not the earrings. And, hey, you have one left—that's something. And for the other ear I will just buy you a flower earring to wear for the hummingbird to land on, but if you're going to be sad about it, you will have to be sad all by yourself."

She decided that it would be worth letting the sadness go and just walk in love with me. I liked that, and we went on. We took a right and started walking down this amazing street of little gift shops. You know, the shops that are so pretty that you can look in to the windows all day long, but there are so many of them that you have trouble figuring out which one to go in first. I had found a few windows and was mesmerized. Then I saw it. I saw the most amazing shaman's necklace. It was just what I had been looking for—the special gift to mark my vacation trip and cap it off perfectly.

A few weeks back I had loaned someone my Tibetan prayer beads that had been blessed by Spirit Doctors and James, a sweet friend of Elia's and mine. I didn't want to loan it out, but I kept hearing this person saying that he was going to come and visit us in a few weeks. In fact, he said, "I might even stay the rest of my life, as we have work to do together, so I can return them then."

I agreed that they were to be returned. I'd had gifts loaned out before that people just decided to loan out to others and then give away instead of returning to me, their owner. To me, that's a lack of respect for self and for the owner who entrusted you to return what didn't belong to you. So please, people, return to others what truly doesn't belong to you.

Not returning something that doesn't belong to you is just stealing.

Unfortunately, I had recently gotten a text from the person with my beads. He had decided that he probably wouldn't be coming to our home, because he had too much to do. Yikes! Not again. Fear. I knew that he was afraid of what he had felt and didn't know how to handle the love he felt for I and Elia. That was that, as we never heard from him again.

I decided that if I would not be getting my blessed prayer beads back, I would find something special and just bless them myself. After all, I was a spiritual healer. I would ask my spirit guides to bless what I could find. I would also ask our friend James to bless it when we saw him again, and I knew that would be only a few months away.

So, we walked. We walked and looked at all of the beauty and saw some of the most beautiful turquoise jewelry; however, I never wear silver and wanted something without the silver. We kept walking, and there it was. But I kept thinking maybe I shouldn't now that one of Elia's hummingbirds had been lost. I didn't want her to feel bad about losing her earring. We walked on. All of a sudden we walked around the corner, and there they were these two lovely people: Damon and Mostafa. They were cleaning the storefront windows of their establishment.

What a soft and gentle soul, I thought. We smiled, and they smiled back. when all of a sudden I said, "Hello," and

Mostafa said back to me, "Yes, hello, could I ask you a question?"

I said, "Absolutely."

"Are you Buddhist?" he asked. I told him I wasn't. "Are you Hindu?" he asked. Again, I told him I wasn't. "May I ask you what, then, you are?" he finally asked.

I smiled and said to this sweet man, "Absolutely. I am Spiritual. I live spirit. I live my truth."

He said, "Would you come into my store so that I could talk with you some more of this?"

I said, "I would love to."

We walked in and listened to an amazing man tell us of his beliefs and wisdom. I and Elia were touched and honored by Mostafa's beautiful soul. What an honor just to listen to him. We stayed in his place of business for fifteen to twenty minutes, talking of our spirit and listening to him tell of his father's wisdom. He would agree with us and tell us more and more of his father's wisdom. His father sounded like he was an amazing man of wisdom and spirit as well.

Mostafa told us about his father telling how bees are always attracted to flowers and honey. We were blessed by his stories of wisdom. He brought to his side his young friend Damon and asked him to listen to our wisdom. He asked us to share with Damon our truths as well. I told him that true riches are within. Yes, money is nice, but true wealth is the wealth of the heart and soul.

Elia and I shared, and Mostafa shared, and we were all blessed together in the peace and quiet of his gem store. We left the shop feeling high. I loved my new friend, and so did Elia. But just before we left, I told them that I had just found out about a brother I never knew—a brother who had died and was never talked about, a brother whom I now new as Manuel. I told them that they could find me on my Facebook with his name and that my site was full of inspirational stuff. I asked them to look me up and keep in touch. They were thrilled and said they would look us up there. Elia and I were thrilled and left the store on a very blessed note.

The heat was wonderful, but Elia needed a ladies' room to freshen herself so we were off on a journey to locate a ladies' room The first person I passed happened to be a local. I asked her, "Do you know where there is a ladies' room?" The woman was awesome with black hair that was tied in about four pigtails on her head, facial piercings, and amazing eye makeup that looked like it was running from the heat (I think that was the look she was going for). I thought she was so cool.

She said, "Yeah right around the corner in the bar."

We thanked her, and she thanked us for asking. I smiled and thought I am sure most people wouldn't have talked to her. I am sure that just because of her looks she had been avoided by many, but to I and Elia , we thought she looked cool and free to be herself.

We walked around the corner and saw no bar; bummer somehow I had missed it. But I walked into the next store, and the ladies there pointed the way to a public bathroom. Yeah! Freshen up city, here we come! The temp had climbed to just above one hundred degrees, and my Beauty needed a splash of cool water to cool her down. Elia went in, and I waited outside. I smiled and nodded to wish the passersby a nice day. It was pleasant passing the time.

When Elia emerged, I said to her, "Let's walk the other street back the same way we came." So off we were to window shop again, soaking in all the sites and the people in the desert heat. We loved it! We looked across the street but found we couldn't bring ourselves to cross it. Strange as it seemed, we just decided to walk back the same way we came—exactly.

We looked and looked, and all I could think about was seeing the necklace again. If it was there, maybe I could get it and replace the one I had loaned out. I was still sad and wondered if I would ever see the borrowed piece again. *Emmanuel*, I thought, *it is just a trinket in life, and you can't take it with you when you die.* The most important thing to tell myself was that the beads were not the power. I was and am the power; the beads were just a symbol. With that, I chose to let it go and walk on.

We were drawing near and no Mostafa, no Damon in sight. I and Elia both thought that would be okay if we didn't see them, as we'd had such an amazing time with them and wanted to hold onto that beautiful moment always in our hearts. We walked past the storefront we had been in with them when I said, "Oh, Elia, that is where that shaman's necklace was. Can we stop and look at it? Would you mind?"

Of course she wouldn't mind. How silly of me, right? Asking the love of my life, "Do you mind if I stop?" So to the store from where we had talked to our friend, we went. There it was. It had all different types of carvings on it: bears, buffalos, lizards, and other creatures of the west and the desert. I was in love with it. I didn't care about the cost; I just wanted it, and I and Elia decided it was meant for me.

We looked up, and guess who was coming through the doorway—Mostafa and Damon. What a joyous sight to behold. They were there because they actually owned both stores; it just happened to be another section of the same place. I was thrilled, and so was Elia. We were able to see our new friends once again.

I told Mostafa I wished that I'd found something in their store earlier to buy just to honor them, but the only thing I had wanted along the path was this necklace. How special I now felt that the necklace was actually at their store. I could honor them by purchasing it. I told Motafa that it looked like a shaman's necklace, and he said that it actually was. I was thrilled, as I told him I was a spiritual healer and it was just perfect for me. I truly felt most blessed in that moment.

We walked into the store only to get to meet his lovely wife, whom the store was actually named after: Chantelle. She was lovely. Mustapha wanted his wife to meet us. We were honored, as we felt like family welcomed into a home of love. What a blessing to meet Chantelle and talk with Mustapha and Damon once again. We talked of spirit and of love and of Mostafa's father once again. We talked of famous people that Chandelle had met and had been able to enjoy time and conversations with. It was lovely.

Best yet for me was when I and Elia paid for the shaman's necklace, Mostafa asked Damon to get a really nice box to put it in. I said, "Oh, Mostafa, I want to wear it out of the store. Trust me. I won't take it off till I sleep at night."

Then honor came when he asked Elia if she would mind if he placed the necklace upon my neck. *He* wanted to put it over my head and upon me for the first time. I wanted to cry as I was being treated with such honor, and I felt such love for this beautiful man. He was honoring me without ever knowing me a day before. He was honoring me because of something he couldn't see but could feel with his heart.

Elia was honored too as he placed this beautiful piece of handmade workmanship over my head. I had chills as he placed it on my neck. I asked him if I could hug him and leave some sparkles on him, and he said, "Of course."

What an honor to have met this gracious, loving man.

Damon brought us a refreshing glass of ice water, and we were on our way. We had left our address in their guest book on the counter. I still hope that they connect with us one day. Connecting would only become a bigger blessing.

We walked back up the street on our way to the motel once again. We stopped again at the ladies' room for Elia to freshen up, as the desert air was dry. But as usual, we are always where we need to be at the right time. Remember the girl who told us about the bathroom at the beginning of the story? Well, there she was, passing by.

I was able to give her a smile again as I yelled out, "Thanks. We found the bathroom."

She yelled back from across the street, "At the bar?"

I said, "No, right here, but you led us on the path to here. Thank you."

Her friend who was with her was smiling and said, "Well, at least you found it."

"Absolutely,." I agreed.

I told them to have a great day, and they both smiled and said, "You too."

All of a sudden, this man in a wheelchair came rolling my way. He had one of those really fancy wheelchairs—the motorized ones. I smiled at him and said hello. He smiled and said hello back.

"I love the weather," I commented.

He smiled and said, "Me too." He wheeled past me and then stopped just a few feet beyond me and said, "Is there a curb drop back there?"

I said to him, "Why yes, sir, there is."

He said, "Oh good," and started backing up. He asked if I was okay, and I told him not to worry. he wouldn't back over me, as I knew how to move out of his way. We both chuckled, and he backed up farther. All of a sudden, out of nowhere, a van pulled right up next to him. The side door opened, and a platform started appearing until it was long enough to touch the ground. The man lined up his chair and started rolling up the ramp.

I said to him, "Well, that's pretty cool."

He yelled back, "Yep, it's rather effective."

Once his wheelchair was in, he spun it around and waved to me and smiled. I smiled back and told him to have a nice day. That was awesome. He was off, and I was really feeling blessed. I had met some remarkable people on my journey that day. I had touched many lives and had been touched *by* many lives.

I and Elia are blessed. More so, we do our best to never let a moment pass us by without giving a kind word to whomever is near us. What does it cost to say hello or to tell someone to have a good day? What does it cost to give a hug to a complete stranger? Nothing but your time.

And what do we all have a lot of in life? Time.

Never let a moment pass
without telling those you
love that you love them.
You never know when
your last moment here is.

Love,
Emmanuel

REALLY I'M JUST A
LITTLE FAIRY ... REALLY

Sometimes to get to the light, we must walk through the darkness, to only find the light was always, within us.

I will never forget the day when someone came to our home for what she said was healing, but the only thing she wanted was to take and take what we had. Although this character in my story is quite real, I choose not to grace her with a name, as I believe that would giver her too much power.

Elia and I were so happy, because we felt spirit showing us to open our home for a place of healing. Now, I know as a healer, everyone wants you to lay hands on them and just make it so. This was not what our home was about. Our home was to be open to the public, so all could come and just be in a peaceful place, feel love, give love, share, and be shared with. Our home is a place of no anger and no judgment, but it's also a place where we don't want anyone else's anger or judgment cast upon us. Our home was, and is, meant to be a place of love—period.

Our first guests had been so amazing; we cried our eyes out when they left. I still wish they had not left, yet love is everlasting; these guests were and are everlasting because of their love.

I knew this other was going to be a different type of guest, as I felt my spirit guides were preparing me for her visit. I was told that we might want this guest to stay out of our home and in the guesthouse. I thought no; we'd met her at a spiritual week event, she'd be fine in our home.

She even announced in front of a large group of mediums, "Emmanuel, I will find you and go wherever you go." With that said, I felt all was going to be fine—just different.

For months I had been shown by my guides that I was being protected from dark or lower energies and that the energies were trying to stop me. I kept asking my spirit guides what they were trying to stop me from doing. My guides would say, "They want to stop you from being loving."

One day during meditation I was not able to see visions like I usually could, so I asked my guides why I couldn't see. My master guide said, "Because we have you in a protective shell."

I asked to see it and was shown I was in an oval energy form that looked like a glowing egg. I looked at my guide and said, "Why am I in this?"

He said, "To protect you from darker energies, so you can grow and do what you will soon need to do. You need to heal and grow right now, and lower dark energies and entities do not want you to do what you are going to do."

I said, "ok" and went back to meditating. I understood what I was being told, as we are all energy on different levels of consciousness. The higher the energy levels the brighter, and the lower the darker. For me, that's a simple explanation.

A week went by, and I still wasn't seeing visions like I was used to seeing, so I said to my spirit guides once again, "Why can't I see the visions like I have been?"

He said, "Because we still have you encapsulated in a protective bubble." I asked him once again if I could see and he said, "We will open the protective energy with a clearing so you can see. *Now* I will let you see." He held me in his hand and showed me inside of this beautiful egg-shaped energy orb. It was beautiful, this energy form, setting in a lotus flower.

When I was finished meditating, I got a piece of paper, found a pencil, and said to Elia, "Look at what my guides say I am in." I felt like a little kid. I showed her the stages of how I was told by my guides that I had been protected. First there was a glowing, egg-shaped energy that I was capsulated in and then, next was an egg form with a lotus flower blooming under it, yet attached as if they were one. The next picture was the lotus opening under the egg shape with four petals of the flower still attached to the top of the egg, leaving an opening so that I could see. At the same time, I was told that the petals that were still attached, kept me safely locked in the safe energy space. I was intrigued. The last picture was me meditating in the lotus position, while the lotus was now completely bloomed under the egg shape, yet still connected.

While telling and showing Elia the pictures, one of our sons, Aubrey, was watching. He said to us at that time, "Does anyone here have an iPad available?"

We said, "Yes in our room." So he left the room to find it.

When he returned, I and Elia were still talking about the drawings and what they could possibly mean. We couldn't figure out, were they metaphoric or were they spiritually real? Who knew. All of a sudden, our son says to us with iPad in hand, "Does this look familiar?" When we looked, he was showing us a photo of exactly what I have drawn he had seen on the Internet.

He told me the story of the orb and how in one of his games, the orb is where the angel of the game puts the character when he is hurt and needs to heal. Aubrey said to me, "Padre, you're in this right now to be healed and protected," and with a "that's cool," he was off.

I was stunned and in awe. I thanked my spirit guides for what had been and was being done for my physical and spiritual growth and safety. So what does this have to do with the title? Everything.

The darkness was still coming, and it was going to do its darkest to stop me from everything I was supposed to do. Over a period of a few months, I was told by many that the darkness and lower energies were going to continue to try their best to stop me from doing what I was to do, and that is to love.

I was still in my protective place, and my guides were working all the time to keep me safe. Our first guests told us they had a few reservations about coming to our home for retreat, as they had felt that my wife, Elia, may still need time for healing from surgery. So, they almost considered not coming until they received an e-mail from us saying, "We look forward to your visit at our Healing Bridge." They told us they were glad that what they felt was not us, as it just felt odd and a bit off.

Well, I will have to say that *these* guests' visit was a glorious event. They came and rested and healed and loved and lived and just enjoyed their visit. We enjoyed it as well. They left, and an ocean of tears fell as we remembered the joy that was still in the air.

Soon after, this new guest would be coming. How exciting, yet I said to Elia, "This visit feels a bit off, but I am sure it will be okay." We made sure to prep the amethyst room. Our amethyst room is a nice room for protection and healing. We filled the room with amethyst crystals, because of their healing energies. Who knew at the time that the amethyst would be protecting us from the darkness?

The day arrived and we knew our guest would be there soon. I and Elia meditated in the temple and felt that this guest would want a schedule and would continually put up a fuss. We felt it would be okay and wouldn't be a major issue, as we would just share, that at Healing Bridge there is no agenda—just time for love, time for joy, and time for healing. I flashed back to the first time I physically met this being and remembered touching her shoulder as I and Elia watched the hair on her neck bristle, but by the end of a week of loving people being together, this person seemed to get better. In front of the crowd she yelled out for whoever would hear that she would follow me wherever I went. So I continued to tell myself all would be just fine.

I was outside working in my flower garden when the energy arrived. I and Elia thought she would have been a bit later, so when she arrived,

I was still a bit dirty from working in the dirt. My favorite pastime and present-time fun, is digging in my flower gardens.

As she stepped out of the vehicle, she started barking orders. Whoa! I looked at her and said, "Excuse me?"

With that, she proceeded to ask a series of questions. "Is this it? Is there more? Well, are there more flowers?" She also wanted to know where and when the sweat lodge was going up and if we had a brochure yet. She explained that she needed and wanted a schedule of the events to come while she was at *our* home.

I was having a moment digesting her commands and demands, when her energy shifted into a nicer tone and she said in a sweet voice, "Oh, before I do anything else, I have something I need to do. I need to give you something for your flower garden."

I blinked and shook my head. I looked at Elia and Aubrey and said to them, "Wow, really?" We were baffled at the sergeant who had arrived and then the sweet little fairy girl who wanted us all to come see what gift she had brought for my flower garden. *Okay,* I thought as I walked over to see what she wanted to give for the flower garden. We stood there quite puzzled by her actions. It was quite a performance to have seen. But, hey, we had met her at the spiritual retreat, and she couldn't be that bad. Right?

The trunk opened, and she began to tell me how she'd bought something for me to always remember her by. She explained that we could just put it in the garden right away so that every time I saw it I would remember her. That was another moment when my mind was saying, *Wow! Really?* Again, I thought, *Well, Emmanuel, it can't be that bad.* And then she pulled out a metal bobblehead sunflower. *Okay,* I thought, *a bobblehead metal flower—not really something I would ever purchase for my garden, but I will be gracious and say thanks and that will be that.* I thought it was over, but she pushed on.

She said to me, "Okay, let's go put it in the ground now. Where can you put it? ... Hmm ... oh look—right over there. You have something over there. See? You can put it there. That will be nice right with whatever you have over there by that little sign."

Well, what I had in my flower garden was flowers and one word, and that word was "LOVE." She was insisting that I put it that bobblehead thing in my beautiful flower garden. I, Elia, Aubrey's thoughts were all together: *what a bossy lady*. Pushy and bossy and still wanting to know what is the agenda was for the day.

I kept hearing in my head over and over to ask her a question. When I finally had a moment, I said, "So, when you leave, what is it that you would like to take from us?" I found the words that I'd heard to ask her to be fascinating. *What did you come to take?*

She rolled her eyes, rudely interrupting me, leaning forward uncomfortably close. "Oh, hmmm ... what do I want to take when I leave? Well, I want to take... what *you* and *Elia* have."

I tell you now that I, Elia and our son were totally creeped out. Chills went down my spine, and I began to feel nauseated. Elia excused herself, saying that she needed to go for a moment, and Aubrey said did the same. I decided it would be best to go to the temple and feel safe for a bit.

Who knew someone was researching how to erode the love I and Elia have? Who knew that someone would actually have an *agenda* to want to try and actually *take* what we had? Guess what, I let her know that she couldn't have what belonged to I and Elia. She would have to get her own, whatever that was, because I wouldn't be giving away what she wanted. She let me know that she had read every detail she could find out about me on the Internet. She wanted me to know that she knew *everything* about me. I let her that know she didn't know anything and that if she were with us to feel our love, then she had come to the right place, as it was a home of peace and healing and love. The tone changed again, and the sweet fairy girl appeared again.

I felt the need to go to our temple.

I entered the temple, took off my shoes, and let her know that we never go in the temple or our home with shoes on. We give the temple and our living space respect. So I took of my shoes and let her know once again that we *always* take off our shoes in the temple. I didn't notice whether she took off her shoes, but what I did notice was that she wasn't interested in hearing *anything* but the sound of her own voice barking, and she wanted her way.

Oh my, I thought, *this is going to be an experience for sure.*

She entered the temple, a place of peace, and instantly started complaining about how awful her life was, how she hated her husband, and how leaving him would be good for her.

I said to her, "I am not here to judge you. I am here to tell you and tell you *only,* I am here to support you in what is loving."

She stated, "Well, leaving my husband *would* be loving."

I remember saying to her, "I am sure you will do what you need to do for love."

"Well, what if it *isn't* loving to leave him?" she asked snidely.

I felt confused. I smiled and said, "Well, if you want to stay with your husband, you will, and if you don't, you won't. I am sure you will do what is loving for you. If you believe you should leave your husband, I will still only support what is loving for *you.*"

She barked back, "Well, I didn't *say* I am leaving him. I *love* my husband."

Are you feeling a bit confused right now? I surly was at that moment. I said, "Then I will support you in doing what is loving for you." I couldn't believe what came next.

"Well," she said with a snap, "I *know* I am going to leave him so I can get what is *mine* and make *sure* he gets what *he deserves.*"

This lady was talking in circles of nonsense, and I was feeling as if I were spinning in a circle. I remember saying, "Well, what do you think he deserves?"

"It's not what he deserves that matters," she said practically hissing. "If I am supposed to be living what is loving to *me,* then what would be loving to *me* is *him* being respectful to *me* and giving *me* what I know I deserve. What *I* want is everything that's *mine*."

As she began telling me all of her demands, her voice started changing. It continued to get louder and louder until she was almost yelling at me. I was in a literal state of shock listening to this *creature*. I kept wondering if it was for real or if I was dreaming. She talked in circles about her demands and kept asking me for *my* approval. She tried to get me in a trap of confusion, but all I could tell her was that I could and would only support her in what was truly loving to *her*. Hurting others for what she wanted was *not* loving, and I would not support hurting anyone.

Wow, did that ever get me in trouble. She barked at me in a spray that came out of her mouth and onto my face. She blared, "*I was told that I can* and *deserve all* that is loving *to me*, and if hurting *him* is loving to *me*, then isn't that *right?*"

Oh my! *Nooooooooo!* But that was not what she wanted to hear. Another round of her arguing came until about thirty-five minutes later when Elia walked in like a breath of fresh air. Aubrey had also crept in quietly. Later he told me that the look on her face and the sound of her voice made him feel like she wanted to hurt me, so he decided to stop in and say hi to make sure I was all right. I was glad they both showed up. I felt the way she was clenching her fists that she *did* want to hurt me.

I was *not* pleased with this visitor. I kept telling myself that it would be okay. She would only be with us for a few days, so it would be fine.

Who was I kidding? Was I trying to go for sainthood? I tell you I wanted to help her, but really there would be no helping her. She had an agenda and more was yet to come.

I looked up at Elia, raised my eyebrows, and said, "I will need to get a shower, as I smell, so I am going to have to part here for a bit." Funny, because most who know me realize that I never smell unless one of two things happens: either I am working really, really hard or I am stressed out. Then I really smell. Well, I was both working hard to keep my head spiritually above water and stressed because each word of wisdom

I shared was challenged with the roar of, "But what is loving for *me* is to get what *I want.*" Oh my, that is not loving; that is not loving at all.

I kept wondering what was going on. *This is not happening, is it?* I showered and felt a bit better. Aubrey walked in the bathroom as I was drying and said, "Well, Padre, you have your work cut out for you. She needs major healing. She's mean and dark, and I can't wait till she leaves."

Another "wow" for me as I looked at him and said, "Honey, the Healing Bridge is for *healing*, not for arguments. It's intended for peace and love and joy. Oh my, this creature, whoever she is, only wants to hurt. So far I have heard that she wants to hurt anything and everything that doesn't conform to her ways."

"When is she leaving?" he asked.

"She says she has enough clothes for a month and will stay as long as she can to punish her husband," I answered. I could only feel that poor man's burden of loving and living with someone so demanding. My heart felt sad for her as I thought for a moment, *Well, I am loving, and she just needs love. I have a lot of love, and Elia has a lot of love. It will be fine.*

Shower was over and I looked out the window and saw Elia and the being walking to the home from the temple. I felt that I needed to get downstairs to make sure the rules of the home were known. I made it down before she made it in.

Now, when you first walk in the home, you enter a beautiful golden room of awe and spiritual beauty. She entered the home and was silent. She started staring at things with squinted eyes as if she were looking for something to complain about. I was already in need of a long, healing meditation; maybe a week at the beach in silence. Instead, I was there, and something very unpleasant had just entered my home.

We walked into the main part of the home, and I explained to her that the kitchen was my personal workspace. I asked that she please respect that space by staying out of it unless she needed ice or cold water from the refrigerator. I realize now that was my first mistake inside the home. Every moment she could, she would walk into the kitchen while I was working with my extremely sharp chef knives and stand next to me, trying her best to get water and ice from the refrigerator. I would ask her to please move, which then gave her something to complain about.

She wanted me to know that she didn't drink any milk, because it would kill her. Aubrey looked at her and said, "Oh, I love milk."

She responded, "Well, like I *just* told you, milk will *kill* me." With that, she looked at me and asked, "What's for dinner? Elia said you would be making a cream soup. Is that right?"

I was astounded that she was still barking—not talking but *barking*. Each time someone would open their mouth to speak, she would say, "But that is *wrong*," or "But that isn't loving for *me*," or "But you don't understand; I would *never* be able to do that." Each word had become a chore with this creature because it was obvious we were not dealing with anything that was loving. We were dealing with something that was on a mission to hurt everything in its path that did not approve of her behavior.

So far she'd made sure she had been planted in our garden. She had made sure we all knew she was not pleased that we were not going to have a list or an agenda to follow. She was not happy that I gave her rules, and one of the rules was to *politely* stay out of my way in the kitchen, and she forced her way to stand everywhere I needed to stand in my kitchen. We were all baffled.

In answering her question about dinner, I said that I had just made a creamed vegetable soup. My eyebrows were to the top of my forehead as she said nonchalantly, "Oh, okay."

I was a bit puzzled… Hadn't she just told all of us that milk would kill her, and now it's okay?

Dinnertime came, and I had made the delicious dinner. I let her know I had put *milk, cream,* and *butter* in Elia's favorite soup.

She said, "Oh, that's fine."

I tipped my head completely confused and said, "Do you want something made for you without milk or dairy in it?"

She said, "No, the soup would be fine."

I was still thinking about her statement to my son that milk would *kill* her if she drank it. So we were at the table, and the soup and dinner and dessert came in. I was so glad that something would be filling her mouth to hopefully keep it shut. When I stated that I would not be putting extra cream on top of her dessert, she looked at me with this childlike pout and said, "*I* don't get any whip cream?"

I said, "No."

We were all confused, but her. Milk would *kill* her, but she had just eaten the *creamed* soup, knowing it was filled with cream, and now she wanted the *extra* cream for her dessert. Darkness had come to our healing center, and darkness was on a mission to take. Every moment it was taking we sat confused, but we were also becoming very alert. I was feeling very blessed for all of my life's training to deal with beings of such dark behavior. I had grown up in a very angry home but never dreamed someone as she would be sitting at my dinner table, staring me down. Darkness was not welcome, but it had found a way in our door and was challenging us.

After dinner, it marched itself out the door and carried its luggage up the flight of stairs while complaining about how long the steps were and how many steps there were for it to climb.

I and Elia and Aubrey locked our doors that night as we slept—too funny, right? I knew I would never be able to sleep with someone of her caliber twenty-five feet down the hallway. With the doors, locked we all felt safe. I kept telling my inner child that this was not my childhood. I could relax, knowing I was safe.

I slept well that night and didn't wake early. I felt so blessed to be in a place where I could be free to rest as long as needed. I had years of never sleeping, so whenever my body slept, Elia would always let me sleep in.

Well, our "dark lord" had been up early and was complaining that she *had* to wait for me.

I woke in my room and saw it was about ten o'clock in the morning.

I felt so blessed that Elia had let me sleep in and rest. I remembered that the day before had been rather stressful. I kept thinking that maybe, just maybe, this person acted the way she had because she was a bit nervous and stressed from wanting a divorce and wanting to hurt her husband and all others who wouldn't conform to her wishes.

My brain was yelling, "Hello, remember me? Are you feeling a bit loopy?" Yikes! It was then that I began to remember the past day with her. Okay, I felt I needed time to meditate before getting a shower and leaving the room. I told myself this day was going to be better. Stay positive; after all, I had left a kind message in a card on the counter to greet her in to the morning. She would enjoy a nice, quiet breakfast and maybe even have a nice meditation out in the temple. Right? Wrong!

I must have been in denial of truths that were in my face and feeling quite delusional to think that she was just having a bad day. Was I kidding? That entity was complaining before I even arrived that morning. When I did arrive, she complained some more to me that she needed a schedule so *we* could all be on it while she was with us.

All the while, Elia was sipping a bit of soda, she wanted us to all know that she and her children never drink soda because it is so bad for you. Did I mention that she was a very large woman at 5' 4" and she also wanted us to know and know for sure that she didn't have an eating problem and that she used to jog with her children.

I laughed inside thinking, *Whoa, you complain of our staircase, you can barely walk, and now you want me to believe that you have been jogging?* Okay, well, maybe twenty years ago she jogged. But, of course, at this time she also didn't have an eating problem. Currently, her ankles were the same size as my thighs, and I was just undernourished at 5'6. Okay, so I'm being a bit sarcastic, but who was she trying to kid? I mean, I used to jog six miles, but that was years ago, and I'm about ten pounds over my suggested weight.

This was someone who thought we were deaf, really, really dumb, and blind too. She—it, whatever—was mistaken. Our faculties were working just fine, and we were watching and asking the universe to help us get her out safely. I was questioning, *How loving are you, Emmanuel?* I realized that to let someone hurt you is a choice, and to me that's not a loving choice. Yes, we would need to find a way to get her to leave.

If you are thinking you need to take a break, just know this *does* end well.

We were blessed to make it through meditation but not before she wore her shoes in, sat in Elia's seat, and then proceeded to let us know she had brought in her journal so she could study and watch us meditate to see exactly how we did it. We did our best to let her know that to meditate, all she had to do was quiet herself and breathe. That wasn't good enough, as she just wanted to watch us and document.

She asked again, "Aren't I *right* for believing that if *I* am doing loving things for *myself I* can hate *my* husband? If loving to *me* is hating *him*, isn't that *correct*?"

Oh my! She was so fixed on twisting what is loving to self. We told her no, and before we could say anything more to explain, she continued. "Well, *I* don't really believe you, because *I* was told it was okay to do things for *me*. *I* was told that if *I* did what was loving for *me*, then it was okay for *me* to continue hurting *my* husband, getting what *I* want and what *I* deserve, and giving him just what *he* deserves for not treating me the way *I* want him to. So what you say just doesn't work, because *I* know what I was told was right."

Now that was creepy. What kind of human being really believes that? *Really!*

I am blessed to say that our heads were on straight. We know in the human existence that there is a difference in what loving is and what hurting others for your own personal gain is. She wanted us to know that black was white and white was black, and we were wrong and she was right. Elia and I blessed the room and began meditating, while she kept complaining about how the crystal she was holding was trying to jump out of her hands. She said that it hurt, because it was burning her. I was having trouble believing that she had just reached over to the temple altar and taken something from it; that was not for her to touch. We asked for protection and began meditation. When the music ended, I was glad it was late. It was time to set out lunch and begin making dinner.

Blessed be, no teaching, let's turn up the tunes and get dinner going. The only thing that could be heard was argument and complaining from this dark source. She was complaining that we didn't meditate at the *right* time so she could meditate with us when she wanted to. Who said she had to meditate *with* us? Not I. She would ask a question, and I would tell her, "You are not here for me to teach. You are here to relax and receive love and let heal what needs to heal." Nothing doing as she would interrupt and tell us again that she was with us to take back with her what we had.

Elia was beginning to feel a bit afraid for us. Me, I was still in disbelief that this was really happening. I had to be dreaming. Nope, it was real, and we were so creeped out by this being. She just stared at everything, squinting, calculating; there were no compliments, no love. She was still, doing her best to gain insight into us to our core.

She blurted out to Elia, "I was told I only have half a soul, ya know."

At that point, we really should have shoved her out the door and sent her on her way, but oh no, sometimes I feel I can save the entire world. She continued with, "I feel I am supposed to be looking for the other half of my soul." She just stared.

"Ya know," she began again, "the love between you two is what drew me to come here."

Elia looked at me, and I raised my eyebrows and looked back. We were not thrilled with what we were hearing and how she was talking. Her voice had become lower, and her eyes squinted again with that calculating look of "I am going to get what I want." We were so filled with, go away.

The creep out meter was screaming, and we were screaming to ourselves to *run*. What was in our home? What were we listening to? This visit was turning out to be a nightmare, and we were the stars in the show. We didn't like it, as it was a very bad show.

I was working with my knife and cutting up veggies for dinner when she decided to try and get around me again. I had already asked her not to come in the kitchen when I was working, and now she was standing next to me while I was using a very sharp knife. Now there are about fifteen other places she could have gone to get water for her glass. While she was holding her bottle of water and trying to maneuver around me, she physically forced me out of her way. I could only think about what a nightmare the situation had become.

Please someone let me wake from this and find it was really just a bad dream. I smiled at her and did my very best to show her that I needed her out of the kitchen, as she took her water, glared at me, and then stormed out of the kitchen. I just shook my head.

Dinnertime finally came, and guess what? She continued to complain that the stairway was too high and that there were too many steps. So what? For her approval I was supposed to build a new stairway in our home? I mean really.

She then continued to tell us that she really didn't sleep very well. She complained that at least she had the flashlight so she could get up, all three times, without falling down the stairwell. She also noted that the trucks in the distance, the train, and cars from the highway almost two miles away kept her awake and that the healing room she was in wasn't working because she didn't sleep at all. There was no pleasing or helping this woman. She liked complaining and hearing the sound of her own voice, and that was that.

I was so glad I had locked my room.

I began to bring the dinner into the dining room as she began her complaints once again. With a snap in her voice, she said, "Well, Chef, aren't you going to at least tell us what you made us for dinner?"

I smiled to her and said, "I do believe that my lovely wife has already told you what was for dinner, and by the way, milk is in the dish."

She shook her hand to me with a gesture of "whatever" to brush it off. I just chuckled and looked at Aubrey, who was leaning quite a bit away from her. Elia was raising her brows to me. I was now saying to this very unique guest, "Are you really for real?"

We began to eat as she decided to take the time to fold her hands like a little child and pray. Now I have no problem with people praying and blessing what they are going to eat. It was the Broadway production she was giving us that rubbed my skin like sandpaper. I looked at her and said, "Just to let you know, the food is fully blessed. I bless it and fill it with love while I cook it."

She just stared at me with a glare as if she wanted to scold me for interrupting her. *We all* (I, Elia, our son) were looking at each other really confused. Our son could barely eat his dinner, and all of a sudden she said in a tiny voice, "So I was thinking about a time maybe we could have a reading."

I smiled and said, "Well, we aren't giving readings right now, as we are focusing on our medium skills to help the living and those in spirit." I couldn't say any more, as she interrupted.

"What?" she said in a very demanding tone. "You're not going to give me the reading I wanted?" Talk about hot under the collar!

I said, "Well, no." We hadn't ever discussed giving readings to anyone. Elia and I wanted to fine-tune our skills for as long as it would take before giving public readings. I looked at her and said, "If you had the choice to hear the truth from Father-Mother-God or get a reading, what would you want?"

She squinted her eyes again, tipped her head, and said, "Well, I would rather have the reading, of course."

I said, "You are *kidding*, right? You would rather have the theatricals than hear the truth of Father-Mother-God?"

She looked at me with her now familiar glare and snapped, "I wanted a reading."

I told her, "Well, I am not giving you a reading, but I will continue to give you truth."

She just continued to interrupt us all for the six hundredth time since she had been with us. Every time we would start to answer her questions, she would interrupt and then say, "Well, *I* don't believe that," or "That wouldn't be loving to *me*." Being selfish, getting what she wanted, and hurting her husband was loving for *her*, and she couldn't see why I wouldn't agree with her. *Really*?

I actually sat back in my chair and quivered. I laughed, but not because it was funny. It was astounding that anything but something dark would think that good is bad and bad is good. She was that dark, and I was astounded that I had been fooled into believing that she was kind and loving. She really had deceived us all. We knew for sure she was not this sweet little fairy, but we did our best and continued to remain calm and focused with love; yet, we were very much aware: We needed strength to get her out.

Dinner was over, and Aubrey had left the room but not the area. He told us later he couldn't stand being near her, as it made him so uncomfortable, so he left the room and listened around the corner to make sure we were never alone. I am grateful, because *then* she started an argument with Elia. She was trying to tell her that she knew Elia was and is like her. "I know you used to hate the old you and have *always* hated the old you," she said. "Only now have you learned to love yourself, but you have always hated yourself until now. Right?"

Elia, as gentle as a lamb and as fresh as the morning air, was fit to be tied, totally flabbergasted. Elia looked at her sternly and said, "I *beg* to differ with you. You are *so* wrong. I have had my problems in life, *but* I love who I *was* and love who I *am*, because with out either, I wouldn't be who I am now, and I love who I am. You are *quite* mistaken."

The creature then looked at me and snipped, "Well, wouldn't *you* agree that if *I* were living to only to be loving to *myself* and to be loving to *me* was to get what *I* want, wouldn't that make *me* right?"

I looked at her and replied, "I have to disagree. You keep telling us that love for you is hurting people. That is so, so wrong, because love is—"

And then she stopped me *again*. This went on for over three hours before she said, "Wow, I am tired and have to go to bed. Look how long *you* kept me up. Gosh, now we can't even meditate because *you* have kept me here so long." Then she added, "So , what are you going to torture me with tomorrow, *huh*?!"

I looked at her in quite a state of shock and said, "We do *not* torture anyone." With that said, it was now 11:30 p.m. Elia and I were exhausted from enduring a dark entity for two days. Plus, we still had dishes to do and a home and kitchen to clean. But I knew *I* would still be going to temple to meditate.

She tried to get out of her chair but was stuck, so she started rocking in order to gain momentum so she could get forward in the chair to stand. The seat cushions on our chairs conform to your bottom when you sit so that you sit more comfortably. She was stuck and rocking and was now complaining that she couldn't get freed from the chair. But once again, she pointed out that she had no weight problem; it was the chair's fault. Apparently, it was just too comfortable. She finally made it off to the side of the chair as she complained and then stood up only to say, "Oh my, look at my ankles. They are all swollen from sitting too long." Are you laughing yet? I am.

I just shook my head. I looked at her and said, "Ya know what? When I look at your face at times, I can see this small fairy-like look. I see someone very small like a fairy trying to balance on one toe while everyone, everywhere is around you holding you up. But that little fairy really isn't what she wants everyone to think she is. She is something totally different. Hmm . . . I wonder what that means."

Before I could finish, she was telling us again that just a few years ago she was running miles and miles, and she was very tiny then. She took us right back to her "tiny," swollen ankles and complaining about how my son would be nicer if he didn't label people. She began to tell us a few more stories about people of other races she knew and saying that she didn't really want to complain about them, but

I stopped her for a moment and said "What about *you* labeling now?"

She responded by saying that she wanted us to know that what she was doing was not labeling; that was her telling a story. *We*, on the other hand, just enjoyed complaining about her. Was this evening ever going to end?

We were ever so blessed when she moaned her way to the bedroom upstairs. We wanted to applaud that she had finally left the room but opted for something peaceful. We celebrated and lit a few candles to bring in the love and light of the universe. Then we did the dishes and picked up the home. As exhausted as we were, we went out to the temple to meditate. We told the universe to "get her out" the next day. We focused and asked all heaven to help assist us in her removal.

Elia then looked at me and said, "Ya know, she did get her way. You did do a psychic reading for her."

She was right. I didn't really care, though. I had given what was needed. I (*we*) had been loving, and now we were using another power—the power of love for us and the power of our intention that the universe would hear and help us.

We finished our meditations. They were filled with love and a greater focus that we had done our best, but this was beyond us. This moment that had come to us was darkness, and it wanted our lights out in every way. We went to bed with our doors locked once again and crystals all around our beds. The next morning, I woke late to an empty bed. Elia had awakened and was about in the home.

Oh my, I thought, *I do hope she is okay.* She was better than okay; she was focusing on the darkness being out and out fast. I showered and walked down the stairs to only hear, "Thank God I'm at least going to be able to meditate at least one more time before I leave."

Oh blessed be, I thought, *we did it. She is leaving.* I smiled and said, "You don't need us to meditate; the temple door is always open, all the time."

Elia said to her, "We will be meditating when Emmanuel is ready to meditate."

I drank the coffee Elia had made for me. Aubrey looked at us and asked us if we were all right and how our day was beginning. I walked back upstairs and had this grandmother talking to me. This was a spirit who wanted to talk to the lady who was leaving. She wanted me to stop what I was doing and go right back down to talk to the woman before she left. So, I finally walked back downstairs

"I have this grandmother here who wants to talk to you." I gave her a name and description and then added, "She has a strong personality; she also loves to work in her flower gardens. She was in her eighties when she died. She says she is your grandmother on your mom's side."

The woman was thrilled she would be getting a message from her grandmother. The grandmother started telling me the message she wanted to convey to the granddaughter. Elia stood by listening to what was told. When the message ended, the granddaughter wanted to disagree with the message , because it didn't agree with what she *wanted* to hear.

"Well, I'm not sure really who that could have been," she said. "That grandmother or whoever was rather forceful, and I am not sure who that could possibly have been. I mean, *my* grandmother wore the pants in the family. When she wanted you to hear something, she got her message through loud and clear, and *you* listened."

At that point I was listening and thinking about how confused I was. *She proved herself to you, and you don't believe that it could possibly be her, even though the spirit acted and sounded like her,* I thought to myself. *But since you didn't like some of what she had to say, then you're not going to believe it.* Yikes! I was done.

I looked at Elia and said, "It's time for me to meditate."

The woman took her notepad to study again. Left her shoes on in the temple, again, and couldn't beat Elia to the chair she wanted. OMG I'd had enough. Candles were lit; incense was burning.

I started prayer and then began meditating. It felt nice and peaceful knowing the darkness was leaving after meditation. I sat in peace knowing her announcement to us was to leave our home after meditation. Awesome.

All of a sudden this little girl in spirit was standing in front of me. She said hi as she poked me in the side, wanting me to laugh. I got the message; I felt as if I were being tickled and start giggling out loud. I said to everyone in the room, "I have this little girl with me, and she is tickling me and wants me to giggle so that's why I am laughing."

Then I heard her say in this sweet innocent voice, "Hi, I am Annie, and I died of cancer." She told me a song, and in my mind I heard it play. Then she said, "My last name sounds like the horses name in the song."

I smiled to her and said, "That's nice Annie."

She then looked at me and said, "Can I talk through you?"

I said, "Sure, Annie." I told everyone listening what was going on, and then I let Annie channel through me and use my voice. She wanted us all to know she liked flowers and that she liked them because flowers represented love to her.

She said, "The flowers represent love to me. Isn't that beautiful?" I told her that was beautiful. She said to us all, "I have a friend with me, and his name is Bobby. He is my pet ferret. He likes flowers too. He bites off the flowers, and I pick them up. Isn't that nice?"

Then Annie said, "That's all now. Bye." At the exact moment she said good-bye to us all, she went to my left through Elia. Elia told me she felt what was Annie going through her. Well, the best was yet to come, because after she said good-bye and went through Elia, she went straight to the stereo and shut off the music playing and the system as well.

I laughed out loud, as we were all a tad startled. I thanked Annie for validating her message. I was so blessed knowing that she was actually there. Since the stereo was about ten to fifteen feet away from me, I was thrilled Annie had shut it all off, as if to say, "Yes, that was me."

The dark energy wanted us to know that that was interesting, but her hand was burning because the crystal in her hand was burning her. Wow, she still had her own agenda. Did she somehow just miss what had happened?

I looked later at a crystal she said was burning her and found it was an amethyst. I had to laugh, because amethyst is a stone that protects, guards against psychic attack, and transmutes energy into love. I had to laugh thinking no wonder she couldn't sleep. She was given the amethyst room that was filled with amethyst crystals. It's no wonder the crystal she was holding was burning her.

I was so taken by surprise when she actually tossed the crystal into the crystal area in the temple—*tossed* it. Wow...

Moments later, she handed Elia a card, told us how wonderful the visit was, and thanked us for how good a time she had. Really, I was so puzzled thinking, *Who are you?*

She gave me a half hug and marched like an angry little child off to her vehicle. She started her car, and after sitting there for a few minutes, waved good-bye and said, "I love you two," and was gone. We knew that was crap but were thrilled to hear the word love in the air as she left. We went inside shaking our heads and screamed with joy thanking the universe she was gone.

Elia walked in the kitchen and opened the card she had left. She left $256 and a notepaper that had "fifty dollars" written on it. We were not sure what that meant. Elia read the notecard, which stated how wonderful and informative her experience was and said she looked forward to coming back one day. *Hmm*, I thought, *not if I can help it; well, unless there is a total transformation.*

The picture on the front of the card was the fairy I had described to her, the one I had seen when I looked at her face. Funny how the fairy looked so nice, but I said to Elia that we all know that looks are deceiving, because the fairy in her was a dark one. She wanted our souls, but that was something that belonged to us, not her. She wanted to test and see if she could drain our every last breath out of us and had wanted to take from us what made us happy, our joy.

We wouldn't give it up. We didn't budge.

I hear people say all the time, never judge a book by its cover. I think I can take that a tad further, because a few days after our little soul-collector left, I wanted some French fries and some tasty chicken tenders. I got out the chicken to thaw and went into our pantry and took some potatoes out of the bin. I pealed one; It was perfect. I peeled the next one, and my wife and I started laughing. The potato reminded us of the visitor who had just left; it was rotten to the core.

It's funny how some people live their truth, while others are only living what they steal, all the while making you think about how beautiful they were. We were presented with the thoughts of "I am tiny; I am frail." All the while, this very large being wanted everything we had, including the light of our souls.

No one, and I say no one, can take unless you give. We learned to be aware and yet remained loving. We remained loving and said no. They say that animals can see bad—the bad we cannot see at times, the bad in others. My wife and I were amused, because when this entity left, she had given us a bush to plant. She wanted us to plant the bush just outside of our door, to symbolize part of her being left behind. I knew that couldn't happen, but maybe we could plant the bush out in back of our home somewhere. For a moment, we thought we could keep it until we let our dogs out of their kennel to run the yard.

They began sniffing and then started barking at the potted plant. Now if you could have seen that moment, you would have agreed that the plant could not stay anywhere on our property—ever. Our dogs were growling and barking at a plant in a pot. Funny how our dogs knew the energy just wanted the thought left behind to grow so we would never forget her, and the thought was there for our dogs to see. We smiled and thanked our beautiful pups. We loaded up the plant and took it off our property for whoever would want it. We decided not to let the plant of bad memories grow here at our home.

We will plant more seeds of love and more seeds of joy and more seeds that all would heal and always walk and be in the light and protection of the spirit of God.

We stopped by our metaphysical store in our area to pick up a few stones we had ordered. While we were there, one of our friends said to us, "Oh my, you just had a dark entity with you for a few days, and you were lucky to escape unscathed."

Wow! She knew. What a lesson for us to see that we were being tested. I've been told I have had enough life lessons, and I agree. I have had my fill. It's time to just love and be loved and be aware. I know we learned a lot from that visitor, as I have told all and all who will listen, "Before you enter the home, you will have to agree to the home rules and sign the agreement, or you will not be allowed in. If you break the rules, you will be escorted out of the home asked to leave."

Love is beautiful, peaceful, and kind. Love is not hurting and wishing horrible things on people just because someone said it is so. Love is a beautiful gift to share. We are all born with the desire to do good, but we are also born with the ability to choose what we want for our lives. Listen to your heart, do good, and be loving to all. We still are, and we know that is who and what we are—*love*.

"If life is what you want it
to be, then why would you
ever want anything that
was not filled with joy?"

Love,
Emmanuel

THE BEAUTIFUL POEM

Someone said to me one day, "Hey, where did that beautiful story you wrote about your ex-wife go? It was so beautiful."

I smiled and said to them, "I think you misunderstood, as the story was about me and the love I chose to be in life."

To begin, I find that people always want to make marriage a contest. You know what? That's not what marriage is all about, or at least that's my opinion. I believe that marriage is a joining of two hearts that love and love each other. I remember someone saying to me, "I and my wife have been together for thirty-one years. Isn't that amazing?"

I smiled and said yes, as I was thinking inside my head, *Wow, if I had of stayed with my first wife that long, I would be bald and have died by now.* Not to say that she was a bad woman. Sometimes the way we are brought up creates quite an event called *us*. If we could all just be raised in the perfect environment with the perfect parents and the perfect pets, that would be grand. But hey, let's get back to reality and realize that life is what you make it, and if you want a happy life, you create it. If you want a sad life, you create it. And if you want a miserable life—then guess what?—you can have that special creation as well.

For me I loved honesty, and my wife didn't. I wanted a peaceful environment, but my wife had been so plagued by her past that she brought it all with her and handed it to me to fix. I guess since I was a spiritual energy worker and healer, she thought I could fix her heart's problems. The truth is what it is, and the answer to being able to fix her was *no*, I couldn't. Bear with the story now as it is filled with love, honesty and truth.

Funny as I read that word *truth*, I remember my wife at that time years ago saying to me, "Why do you always need to be so truthful? Maybe sometimes you should just lie to me." For me that was a definite no. I was raised in an abusive environment but chose not to be what the past taught. I always believe that the past is the past for a very good reason, and it should stay right where it is—behind me.

I can remember my oldest being so angry at me for about two years after I was divorced from his mother. He kept saying to me, "Padre, you can fix everything, so why don't you fix your marriage?" I did my best to show him that if two are meant to be together, they will stay together, but if two are meant to be apart, they will go their separate ways. That wasn't good enough for him, so I cut to the chase and said, "My son, I cannot fix another human heart. I can move energy and influence, but I cannot fix someone. Only they can fix what they believe needs fixing. It's like asking me to fix a drug addict who doesn't believe he has a problem. It will never work." Eventually, he got it when he married someone just like his mother. He thought that he could fix her until two years after his wedded bliss. By then, his wine had turned to lemons, and the pucker in the lemon juice was blaming him that its lemon essence was sour.

In this day and age, I hear so much about family values and that good old contest called marriage. I think it would be so much better if we would just learn how to love each other more as a human race and move forward together, rather than saying only those in a certain little club of judgment can get a contest card for marriage. Love is love, and marriage should *always* be a union because of love and not duty to serve.

Someone said to me once why I was divorced. I explained that it was because it was time to move on. Did I love her? Yes, but sometimes love is not enough to keep as the glue for two people to stay together. The love needs to be mutual.

In the beginning, I was her love, and she was mine; that was why we needed to be together. I remember one day my then wife coming to me and asking me to do that thing I had always done for her. She would say,

"I don't really believe in what you do, but whenever you put your hands on me, the pains in my head always go away."

She asked me to check a spot, a lump, on the back of her head and see what I thought. I told her that I am a healer, but not a medical surgeon. I knew she would need the lump looked at right away. I knew she needed it removed as soon as possible. She had a doctor check it out that week, and within that week, she was in the hospital having the tumor removed. The doctor wanted her to know that if it had of grown any larger and spread into her brain, it would have killed her.

Shortly after that, the divorce came. I believe she needed my love to sustain her to that point and I was always happy to give it. She was always too stubborn to see a doctor, but I was insisting at that time and I know that saved her life. Now, will she ever remember the love that watched over her, or will she choose another term for me? Don't say that term. Frankly, that's none of my business to know. Her life belongs to her, without me, and my life is mine for me to continue as well. I know that as spiritual beings, we have lessons with others. When those lessons are over, they are over, and we need to move on and grow. I know if we take our pasts with us, we make the past the present and I believe that is a very sad and painful sight. I can never forget it, but I can leave it where it belongs—way behind me.

I wish for her growth, healing, and love in her life. I wish that she could remember one day that love was always with her. I know what she was, and that was the past. I know the same goes for me, and that is the past too. I know I choose love and move on and to be in the present, so remembering the poem I wrote— that was me then. This is me now—the same but better, loving and moving on in my walk of life's lessons and love.

Yes, it was a beautiful story, and it was my past. Now that I am in the present, I am here to tell you still that love is the greatest energy in the universe—love. So to all the couples who want to blame each other and continue the bitterness year after year— let it go and bring love into the moment of now. Just let it go and let the spirit of love consume you.

A bit of time later, I and my true love found each other, and I would not miss a day of her sunshine for anything in the world. For all of you who are looking for love, you'll find it. For those who married and found yourself in a divorce after twenty-five years, remember that may have just been a place to stay to help a friend you loved, while the love of your life found you.

Here's the poem:

> There's a song that's playing in my heart
> And I'm not sure where to start,
> But I remember a long time ago
> I took your hand and loved you so.
>
> You looked at me and I looked back,
> A life began and that was that.
> We had a lifetime six kids plus more,
> My heart became the grocery store
>
> And then one day we grew apart,
> The time was over, for new to start.
> Yes there was that pain that, we both felt,
> We wanted more for us: our wealth.
>
> And so the separation began,
> I was me and you were Sam.
> That's how it's started and ended too,
> There was no friendship; there just was blue.

An overwhelming sadness, uggg we forgot,
That in our lives we had a lot.
We had six children to share in love,
We had a home, it fit like a glove.

Oh time has gone forgiveness flew,
Time had wings between me and you.
The more we tried the further they went,
It seemed that the love from us, all spent.

Then for me my guide he said,
This contract of the heart, 'tis over my friend.
Let go, let go, for more to fill,
You know the routine, it's called a will.

Whose will are you choosing, just let it go,
Live for love, let it flow.
I died that day, I cried for you,
When I knew I loved you, I knew what I knew.

And now that life's over, but I still love you dear,
It's just that it's different, no longer with fear.
I grew up and grew past it, I couldn't heal,
The layers of life you would reveal.

But it just doesn't matter, six kids we still have,
And now there's grandchildren, oh let us be glad.
Dad, he did visit and with me, he shared,
He said to me, let it go, I know now You Cared.

And that day I freed ME,
I let my heart open
Returning he gave me.
St. Lucy the ocean

My mind it healed down there,
I felt the bright sun
I remembered the times
Our life shared as one.

Dawn's blooming brought to me
A beautiful light
And there it was standing
A beautiful sight.

So to you forgive
For I couldn't heal,
The part that you wanted
So that you could feel.

And for you I wish this
That, you'll find your way,
Whatever your journey
Whatever your day.

Just know that I loved you
And know I still do,
And love was the gift
Between me, between you.

THE VISITORS

For weeks, I had been doing my best to be patient for things in life to get better. We had traveled and had been alone to only have an amazing time. We were told by a few psychics and mediums that something was going to try to stop me from doing a job I needed to do. Elia and I were beginning to feel the effects of negativity and low energies around us—what we call "spiritual vampires." Our prayers and mantras were to only attract all that is perfect, holy, and loving. We wanted to open a loving healing center for people to come and heal and feel love.

We had so many people at that time coming into our path and doing their best to stop us from feeling happy, peaceful, and holy and doing their best to distract us from doing what we felt we needed to do. But that actually seemed to strengthen us. It seemed that all the while insanity was occurring around us, we were becoming stronger.

We had moved to our home in New York from our little spiritual nest in Boston and were feeling a bit confused about our life's direction. I said to Elia, "What the heck is going on?" Some of our friends at this time were telling us that we were not asking for the right things for our life, and if we were still attracting dark energies, then we weren't focusing 100 percent on what we wanted correctly.

Okay, I don't know about you, but I really wanted to tell these people that they were full of crap and had no idea what they were talking about. I know I only wanted love, support, and protective light and not their judgmental opinions, which I was doing my best to just ignore.

As a child, I was told in spirit that I was a soldier for God against the darkness. Hmm that was quite a thing for me to swallow as a child. Imagine trying to explain to people when I was younger that I knew I was special. You get really tired of the ridicule from your peers really fast. Hey, they knew that I wasn't that special—at least that's was what I was told.

My mind knew better, so I learned to be silent about that special thing. I would hear, "You're no more special than anyone else" or "Well, my children are special too, so there." I was always so amazed. I just wanted to share how wonderful I felt. I carried that with me my entire childhood but learned to keep it quiet.

As an adult, I grew to care for myself better. Though my first wife would say sarcastically, "You're special all right," my second wife would now say to me, "Babe, do you know how special you are? I could see it in my Elia's eyes—she knew.

Wow, for me, my life was finally feeling fulfilled. I had a beautiful wife who cared for me like I had always felt inside—beautiful, happy, loving, and special to the core.

So finally our home was cleaned once again from our last guests. We had saged, cleansed, and prayed and meditated over it, doing our best to clear the energies from the last visitor. Our last visitor wanted to shake us and test us. She left us a dirty T-shirt under the bed with a message of "I am still here with you." We cleaned *everything* and made it tidy for our new visitors, who were coming soon.

I had to do a bit of extra clean up too, because I had been doing artwork on the walls with crystals. I love creating as much beauty as I can everywhere I go. I had been using industrial-strength hot glue, gluing rose quartz crystals to the wall in the shape of a heart and then surrounded that with an amethysts border. Yes, this was on a bedroom wall. Our amethyst room was becoming more stunning every day. When our guests come to visit, I and my wife always want them to feel healing energy, love, protection, and everything else that is good loving and spiritual.

My hand got scalded that night I assembled the heart, but because I am a healer, I and Elia went to the temple to meditate to ask for healing assistance from our spirit doctors. We were really being pushed around by dark energy, but I refused to yield to it, so out to meditate we went. I asked that during the meditations our spirit doctors would come into the circle and assist in healing the scalded spot on my hand.

Elia was so upset, as it was very swollen and very red. We started meditations, and I did what I do and relaxed and let go. About thirty minutes later, the music stopped, and I said to my wife, "Well, let's go to bed. We have to get ready for guests coming again." We had forgotten that I had even been burned. Now letme explain. My thumb and the palm of my left hand had been scalded by hot glue that was *bubbling*, and I was unable to get it off until it had cooled. It was a *very* bad burn.

So to catch you up again, our meditations were over, and we had forgotten about the burn. I reached to Elia with my left hand, and she took it. We walked out of the temple across the driveway to our home. We walked inside and got everything ready for the next day. She took my outreached hand again, not remembering that the left one that had been scalded, and we walked up the stairway and started toward the bedroom. We were exhausted, as it was about one o'clock in the morning. All of a sudden she said, "Oh my God! I have been hurting your hand! Isn't this the hand that was just burned?"

I started laughing and said, "Well, actually, it was. But look, it no longer hurts. It has a *blister*, but it no longer hurts."

We were both so amazed and happy to boot. She touched it, and I touched it as well. I must say that it was an awesome moment. I know burns as I was burnt as a child; seventy-five percent of my body with boiling hot water, so I know all about burns and how long it takes for the pain to go away—forever. But the pain was *gone*, and we were both thrilled. I thanked spirit over and over till I fell asleep that night. I remember thinking what a blessing it was to be in such a beautiful and holy place.

I woke the next morning with a mission. We had an errand to run and one last task to do before our guests arrived. I was going to pick up a piece of kunzite, which, to me, is a rather protective stone. I was told by my guides to get it and bring it into the home. Well, we made it to the store and found everything but the kunzite, so I was off to another store to see a piece that I knew had been waiting just for me. It was a ring, and wow, it was beautiful. I had hoped for a necklace, but hey it was beautiful, and it called my name. I knew it was waiting just for me.

Believe it or not, the ring had been on hold at that store for two years. I was told, "Wow, you are looking for kunzite? I have had one on hold. I wasn't sure why, but I knew I needed to hold it."

I was glad too, because it was perfect. I asked if the ring could be sized to my finger, and the beautiful man said, "Absolutely." I was thrilled. Unfortunately, my darkness dispeller and protector ring was not going to be able to be with me for a few more days while it was resized.

My children and a few close friends were adding us to their continual prayer and meditation list. We were thrilled. More positivity is always a good thing to add to one's life. When we finally arrived home, I said to my wife, "Were they talking about a storm at the store?"

She said, "Oh, I don't know. It must be going to rain."

I didn't care if it was going to rain; I just needed to ready the home for the new guests. I kept hearing my father, who is in spirit, say to me, "It is important for these people to meet you." I felt a bit anxious about them coming, but I pushed it off. I wanted to make sure everything was perfect, clean, and blessed.

We had one day left before their arrival, as they were driving from Florida to New York State to see and meet me. Whoot! How lucky can they be, right? Yes, they were coming to meet both of us, but the visit was to meet me in this place of holiness, love, and healing.

After we got home from the store without the kunzite, I walked upstairs and started to sweep the floor of the room that was being prepared for our special guests. You see, all of our rooms are set up for special purposes. Tragedy of the heart is the rose room. Peace is in dad's room. Earth energy is in the garden room. Healing and protection is in the amethyst room. I think you get the drift, right?

Well, I started the sweeper, and the power kicked off. At the time, I had no idea that we were having a storm outside. All I knew was that I was a man on a mission to get the room clean for our guests. I gave a scowl and said to spirit, "Come on, really? I just need to get this room ready for the guests." With that, the power kicked back on, and I started to sweep again. As I continued sweeping, the power kicked off again. I was grumbling once again, "Come on, guys, let's keep the power on. We're going to have guests."

Elia looked out the window from where she was standing and said, "Oh, this must be the storm they were talking about at the store."

I smiled and said, "Well, it doesn't look like it's that much, as it's just raining a bit, so I wonder why the power keeps going out."

When the power kicked back on, I hurried so I could get the floor in the room prepared for our guests. *Yes,* I thought the room was finished, and instantly there was a boom and no power. I thought to myself, *You are kidding. Did the transformer just get hit again?* There was another flash of light, and the power and lights went out again, but this time they didn't return.

I said to my wife, "Sweetie, would you call our daughter in Boston and find out what is going on?" Now, I must let you know when we built our home, I designed it to have thicker walls to add more insulation, more soundproofing, and better heat and cooling control. We felt blessed that when the windows were closed, nothing was heard from the out of doors. We were beautiful, safe, secure, and fairly soundproof in our home. We finally reached our daughter only to find out we were having a tornado. Surprise! There was the storm.

"A tornado?" I said. "And why can't I hear a sound?" From where I was standing, it didn't look that bad. I walked to the front door and started to open it, and as the seal around the door began to break, I could hear a hiss forming. Hmm... something was obviously going on, so I pulled open the door.

Now, I must add something here before I go on. In all of my meditations, I always ask that our home and property, above and below, are protected and safe from all harm. It's just a thing with us here at our home.

So, I opened the door and quickly saw that, yes, my daughter was correct. A tornado was going on. We now watched as masses of leaves and branches snapped off of the trees. Rain and heavy winds surrounded us, and yet all of the damage seemed to be occurring around the edge of the property.

I say to my wife then, "Hey Elia, have you noticed that the storm isn't really bothering us?" It seemed to be affecting everything outside of our property. We stood on our porch for a bit watching the storm, amazed at what was going on. The trees were actually bowing out, not in.

Finally, we went back in and realized how well insulated and well built our home was and how blessed and kept by spirit we were. I will tell you I was a bit disgusted that we had no power, but I felt that it would be on soon enough, so no worries. We decided that since we couldn't do anything else, we would go out to the temple and meditate.

We looked around, and all we saw were leaves—no damage to *anything*, just leaves on the driveway; nothing out of place, just leaves. I had heard a large tree about the size of my waist snap in two near our side yard. I'd heard many small trees and branches fall, but there was no damage to us.

We gave thanks to the universe and went out to the temple to meditate to bring peace and thanks to our hearts. We were thrilled to have a battery-operated stereo for our meditation music. We turned the player on and meditated. About an hour later the storm was calmer, and we were done with our meditation.

The time had come to have another reality check. Even though we were calm and guests would be arriving the next day, I was having a tad bit of anxiety knowing that I was the cleaning force and was without electrical power to do what was needed. After all, we would be having four adults and three children, all under the age of six and a half. We would not only be needing a clean place, but we would need operational bathrooms and the kitchen would be needed, especially the refrigerator. No refrigerator would mean no food, and no power to run the fridge meant spoiling food soon.

Okay, I kept thinking, *it is all going to be fine. I'm supposed to trust that all will be okay. So, power, where are you?* My wife called the electric company and found out via a recorded message that the power would be back on in a few hours. We felt a tad better and sat on the porch, relaxing and waiting for the hours to pass. We ate dinner by candlelight and shared some lovely quiet time together. Still, I couldn't stop think about hearing how darkness (lower energies) wanted to stop me from doing what I needed to do, and now we had no power and all I could do was wait. But the power company did say the power would return soon, so I felt that patience was in order, and we both need not to worry and just relax.

Well, the time came and went, no power. A few hours later... still no power. We finally called the power company again, and the recording said, "Due to the damage in your area, over four hundred are without power in your area and at this time, there is no estimated time of getting back power."

What? I thought. *You've got to be kidding, right? I am supposed to be trusting and laid back and still no power.*

It was now eleven o'clock at night—no power, no water, no bathrooms, just a lot of no's. We decided to go back to temple to meditate. We knew that we needed to meditate and pray for the lines to be repaired quickly; otherwise, there would be a lot of food spoilage. Our refrigerator and freezer had just been filled to the brim, because guests were arriving the next evening. I and Elia were filthy and hot in the 90-degree humidity. We could at least get a cool breeze and no more rain to fall so that we could keep the windows open.

Our daughter had told us it was supposed to rain all night, but we took a chance and opened the windows in just our bedroom. We cleaned up a bit with what water we had and went off to bed. We were so thrilled that we had our iPods and phones charged so we could do our evening meditations in bed and bring love and light to the area where we lived. It didn't cool till halfway through the night. I had left a fan on in hopes that the power would come on and cool us off, and it would all be over.

The next day came, and still we were without power. The tornado had done a lot of damage.

Even without any power, I and Elia actually had a good morning. It was a tad tense, but we had some water and made a small pot of coffee (thank goodness we had a gas stove), had a few chips, and decided to do what we could to either get ready to leave or get ready to continue to clean the home without power and just do the best we could.

At times, it is hard to explain things that happen to us, because they are often so unbelievable to so many. For example, glasses, plates, and bowls falling off shelving when nothing but spirit is there, or glass breaking everywhere, lights turning on and staying lit because spirit wants them on, or stereos shutting off because a spirit wants to make a point. This time, however, it felt as if a source was pushing us out of our home because it wanted us gone, but we couldn't put your finger on exactly what was going on as it was all so subtle.

Ya know, like every fifteen minutes or so something would shut off because the battery would run out. Fifteen minutes later I'd find a pile of dirt that I couldn't clean up because the broom was missing. All this time the food was thawing, so I had to race the clock and pray I had enough ice to last till I could either get more or take the food to another home, and all the while, I didn't realize my head was spinning in a whirlwind of thoughts. Then, at the same time, my wife was going through the exact same thing. While not wanting to sound silly, neither of us told the other, so we each felt we were going just a bit crazy. You know the feeling?

When I got off the phone from another call to the electric company checking up on the estimated time for repairs recording, I finally said to my Elia, "They are no longer having estimated times of when they think the electricity will be on. If we can't get power, we can't have guests and even though I really know we should be with these people, we will need food, water, and bathrooms for all but without power, we won't be able to have them."

I know we were both feeling sad and frustrated, but what could we do other than wait? We decided to clean out the refrigerator and see how the frozen foods were holding up. Elia went to get ice, while I started to clean the fridge. It was frustrating seeing all that had already gone bad in the heat. My heart ached at the thought of all the money we had spent just a day or two ago to have everything ready for guests and now we might have to throw hundreds of dollars in food away, take what we could, and run from the storm and its aftermath. I was not happy, and I knew Elia was not either.

She came home with a cooler and some ice and said, "Well, if we are staying, we had better put the cooler and ice in the basement and protect it all from the heat. I stood looking at all that we already had to throw out and felt tormented about what to do.

Should we stay and hope for another day? What if we stayed, and there was still no power? What a mess it would be to be waiting for power with our guests. Should we pack up, give the guests a call, and say sorry but it's going to have to be another time?

We packed our cooler full to the brim with as much food and ice as we could. The refrigerator freezer was no longer going to be able to hold our frozen food. Water was now leaking all over our kitchen floor. Oh yeah... another mess to clean up. Maybe this was just a message to leave. I felt this presence pushing us to leave, and I finally said to my wife that I'd had it. I kept asking what to do, but all I heard was silence.

Elia looked at me and said, "Yes, that is all I am getting."

We were on stress overload. Maybe I should have gotten the message and done nothing since that's what I was getting but, oh no, not me. I needed to do something. It was okay, though, because I said to my wife, "I am going to go to the storage barn and get a bigger cool. We are going to get more ice, fill it up, and leave here." I felt we had to go to our Boston home anyway, as we would be traveling to Georgia in about two weeks, so we would leave early and at least have the luxury of electrical power and all that comes with that. The guests would have to come another time.

Funny how we started to make phone calls and couldn't get through, but we were going now. That was that. We made a decision. I had decided to go outside, get the car ready, then pack, and go. I'd started preparing when one of the guests called my wife's phone. They were stuck two hours away in heavy traffic. They had heard the news, and as disappointed as they were, they guessed that they would have to agree that without power it would be best for the seven them to come another time. They would just go somewhere else and visit our home another time. We were all saddened but had made a decision.

I stomped outside totally irritated with disappointment that we wouldn't be able to talk with them and allow them to feel the healing that walked and echoed in the halls and rooms of our healing home.

I walked back inside and looked at my wife, as I knew what was up. She was shifting, as I put it. At any given moment, she was going to be channeling someone in spirit. I never knew who; I just knew it was going to happen any second now.

All of a sudden, this deeper voice of my dad came booming through Elia. He was yelling to me, "You can't go! Don't you know that we need you? You have a job to do, and these people *need* you. The community here *needs* you. *Don't* abandon *us*; you have already come so far."

I could have really let the ego run amuck, but if you know me, that doesn't happen. My childhood gave me the strength to always put the ego where it needed to be and that, for me, was out of the way.

"We *all* need you," he continued. "You know who you are, and so do we. You know how powerful your love is, so *why* aren't you doing something about it? *Why* are you letting darkness run you out?

"I *know* you. I *know* how strong you are. I *always* knew you were strong, and now I know even more how strong you are. People need the energy you emit, the energy that you are. You ripple that out *every day,* and people need to feel that for their consciousness to grow. You cannot run; you must stay. I know you will listen to me, because I know that you *know* and *stand* for the truth."

With that he ended the visit with, "You must stay, you know it, you must. Take the power that you are—the love that is you—and *do* something about your situation. You are the most powerful being I know, so *do* something. Don't just sit there griping; *do* something!" With that, he ended the visit.

I barked back and screemed to him, "Okay!!! If *you* think I need to do something, then *you* have to help me! *You've* got *one hour* to help me, or I am *out* of here! Got it?"

That said, I looked my wife and said, "Elia, I need you to drive to Appalachian (a town about twenty minutes away) and get us two barbecued chicken dinners. While you are gone, I am going to do what I know how to do—heal, manifest, love, and meditate. I told my dad I would give him one more hour, but he will have to give me some proof that we really need to be here and help me out."

I kissed her good-bye, and she was off. I waved till she was out of sight (as is always my tradition) and then off I went to my temple. I lit some incense, lit the candles around the altar, and started my breathing exercises. I opened up my chakras and started focusing on energy balls of light to heal the *dis*-ease in the area (note the *dis*-ease and not disease). I focused intently for a few minutes till I felt the energy vast and dense. I then imagined that when I sent out the energy, it would be like a sonic force—a sonic boom—like that of an explosion, but this would be a healing energy sent forth by the power of love.

As an artist, I could see what I was doing inside my mind's eye. It felt good to be focused again and not feeling the chaos that we had been feeling—that feeling of run, run, *run*. My heart wanted to stay but for what? Nothing was working but *me*. Nothing was working but the love that resides within Elia and me. I stayed focused for what felt like about ten minutes as I sent out healing shock wave after healing shock wave, over and over again until I heard a car door shut. I opened my eyes, and there was Elia outside. She had already returned from her errand.

I smiled to her and said, "Wow, you're back already."

She acknowledged me and said, "Well, it's been almost an hour."

I told her it only felt like ten minutes or so. No matter, I did what I had needed to do, and I was waiting for my dad to show me some proof. I needed proof that I was supposed to stay for guests. I said to my wife, "Let's go inside and eat our dinners. Let's relax a bit while we are waiting for whatever to happen." And if nothing happened, we were ready to return to Boston.

We had only just gotten in the door and taken a bite out of our chicken when we heard something. I had the kitchen window open so I could hear the truck engine nearing us. I stood and looked out the window to see one of those very large electrical trucks with one of those huge buckets on top pulling up out back of our home.

Elia and I walked out and said hello, and Elia asked if they'd been able to find the problem yet. They didn't hear us, so they walked toward us and said, "Pardon?"

Elia looked at the gentlemen and repeated, "Did you locate the problem yet?"

This very nice, taller gentleman looked at us both and said, "Well, I think if all goes well, I will have power for you in the next *hour*."

I could hear what I'd said to my dad ringing in my ears—he had *one hour*. This guy was repeating those words right back to me. I walked back in our home and I said to Elia and my dad, "Okay, I will give you your hour, but if nothing happens after that, I am out of here." I looked at Elia and said, "Do you hear me, Elia? One hour. Right, Dad?"

I decided to keep busy, so I mopped the floor by hand, and Elia and I picked up the rest of the home the best we could. We finished cleaning what we could and then sat by candlelight to finish our dinner. Hot, sweaty, and rather dirty, but content to wait out the hour. We had about three or four minutes left when all of a sudden the lights flashed and then just quick as they went out, *boom!* They were on once again. Blessed be! Dad had proved himself once again. We would stay. *Thanks for the message, Dad*, I thought. *We needed that.*

The next part of the miracle of what happened was just as beautiful. I said to my wife, "Well, if we are lucky, we might be able to catch our guests before they are out of the area." I remembered that the last time we had talked, they said they were two hours away and in slow, heavy traffic. We called and got through. It was exciting reconnecting.

We asked them where they were and if they were still near our area. They let us know that they had just as we called turned on the road to go away from us and asked why we wanted to know. We told then our power had just turned on, and they were welcome to come if they still wanted to. They wanted to and told us they were on their way. I smiled and said, "Good timing, Dad." I thanked the universe and all the spirit beings that were doing their best to bring us electricity and two cars filled with guests.

We had just enough time to get the rest of our floors swept, and I was off to the showers. I had just undressed when all of a sudden I could hear horns tooting, voices cheering, and laughter everywhere. I looked out my upstairs bathroom window and yelled a beautiful welcome to our home, our Healing Bridge. Tears filled my eyes, as they all wanted to know why I wasn't at the door. I shared that I had just undressed and stepped in the shower only to hear horns and voices, but I would be down with Elia as soon as I could. Really, I needed to at least get my pants on!

It was beautiful as the door opened, and for the next ten minutes, hugs and laughter was all that filled the air. I will share that there were a few tears of joy amongst the group. So why did my father want me to be with this group? What was so important for me to share or hear or help with? I walked the grounds with one young man and some of the children. We laughed and shared and loved and hugged.

The group had stopped along the way and bought two sheet pizzas since we hadn't time beforehand to prepare dinner for them all. We walked to the front porch so they could eat, and then I took a few of them on a tour throughout the home. They had heard what I was doing with the crystals and couldn't wait to see. It was a wonderful venture and a great learning experience for the three children, as I asked them not to touch the crystals, as they were working and doing a job for us. I let them know that they could rub all of the Buddha bellies. They loved that. It was so priceless when the oldest one said to me, "I can touch the Buddha belly? Is it because he is not crystal?" His mom and I smiled and told him yes.

It had been a few hours since they had arrived, and I still had not gotten a shower. I was feeling a tad gross. So I excused myself while my beautiful, loving Elia filled the spot as the gracious host and continued the conversations. I showered and felt much better. Being together with human beings, you know, hugging and sitting close to people, you want to be clean. There was going to be no perfect first impression for me. I met them filthy. It was take-me-as-I-am day, and they loved it.

Finally clean, I stepped into my bib overalls, dried my hair, and opened my bathroom door. Hearing voices in the hallway, I invite the visitors to come and visit with me if they would like. This lovely young lady, her son, and her dad peeked their heads around the door, and I told them it was okay. If they wanted to step inside my private space, they could, as I was dressed, clean, and all ready to visit and love once again.

Within a few minutes, the young lady and her son were off to find her other two children, her loving beau, and her mom, but dad stayed behind to visit. The visit was heaven to me, as every time I looked at him I could see the loving eyes of my dad looking back at him. Seeing my dad in him brought tears to my eyes. I told him that his cheeks and eyes looked just like my dad and if I knew him just a bit more I would grab him, hug him, and just cry on his shoulder. He chuckled a bit and asked me, "So I look that much like you dad, huh?" I answered that yes, he did.

We began to talk and found that both of our lives were filled with pain and abuse. Our dads hadn't meant to be abusive. That was just the world they knew and thought was right. We talked about it and felt a bond between us growing. Those words weren't shared, but I knew it was so. I was now beginning to understand why these people were here. Yes, they too needed healing, and they too needed rest. They also needed the healing hands of spirit touching them helping to ease the pains of the past, while I was there to bring them into stories of forgiveness and healing and bring them into the present for understanding.

We both found that we had the same type of upbringing. You've heard it before: spare the rod, spoil the child. I think my parents in general could have spared the rod a lot. I think his dad could have too. We talked about how we cannot blame others for the past, as it is what it is—the past. To bring the past with you only makes the past the present, so you always need to be willing to let it go. We talked of having the same number of siblings and both of us having one die in life to live with us now in spirit. We smiled, how much our stories rang the same. I was able to then share with him what happened to all of my *dis*-ease when I was able to heal with my dad and let it all go.

I told him of an ulcer that was no more. I told him of a bloody, crackly psoriasis all gone within a few weeks. No more crutches and canes because of blood clots. I told him of no sleep to sleeping now. From hair loss to hair gain and living with someone whom I felt was amazing and fantastically special—*me*. I shared with him the story of scalding my hand. He reached forward and touched it as he asked when it happened and then apologized when I told him it had only happened the day before; he thought he might have harmed me. I smiled and told him no worries as it had healed; there was no pain.

He was amazed—and I was too—that we were enjoying a conversation. I was also enjoying healing someone without them even realizing it was happening. That was spirit's plan, for our energies to just stand together. I was touched deeply by remembering my dad pleading with us to stay. My venture had not ended with them, as within the next moment a small young man who had pain and sadness in his heart came to me. His name was Ryan. He was a small little guy about six and a half years of age, and his heart was filled with pain and sadness, as he wanted his mommy and daddy back together.

Life has its lessons and choices. Sometimes the lesson is to learn to love someone else and understand we all have choices. Sad to say, this little guy was so young he just wanted the pain and sadness to just go away. I could see it all over his face. His energy was filled with a sorrow that radiated all around him. I and Ryan went to our temple, and when we got inside, Ryan and his stepdad were mesmerized by all the crystals and all of their beauty. I explained that crystals were my work tools, and I would appreciate they not touch them, but let them do their job and radiate healing energy to all.

I began to share a story with Ryan about a very dark lady who came and wanted only to take what we had. I told him how she told me, "I have come to your home to *take* what *you* and *Elia* have." His eyes grew very wide as he started listening intently.

"Wow, was she ever creepy," I said. "Yet, creepy as she was and is, she had a job. At that moment, it was for me to be aware and be alert and be on my toes. I guess you could say her job was helping me fine-tune myself, like the crystals."

So I told him how she reached into the altar and took out an amethyst wand crystal, and all of a sudden she was tossing it in her hands and complaining how she couldn't hold it and how it hurt to hold it, until all of a sudden she said, "Ouch! That hurts; that *burns*," and she tossed the crystal three to four feet away back onto the crystal altar, fracturing it badly. I told him that is why we ask people not to touch the crystals.

At the same time, I told him because she was of a dark and lower energy, she couldn't hold the crystal, and that is why she felt it burning her. The crystal was doing its job and protecting us from her. His eyes were getting wider, as at that moment he had begun to lean away from me and the story.

I reached into the altar and took hold of the crystal and said to him, "Do you know what I want you to do? I want you to hold this crystal and let it help you." I told him if he was willing to let go of the pain he was feeling inside, the crystal would help remove the pain and sadness in his heart, and like a sponge, it would absorb his pain and sadness and leave a space for joy to fill.

Funny thing happened next. He was listening so well that the main thing his child's mind heard was how the bad, ugly witch-lady got burned by the crystal, and he didn't want to get burned like she did. I said to him, "Here, let me put this in your hand so it can help you."

But the only thing he was thinking was, *I am going to get burned, because I have been bad too. I have been so bad that my mommy and daddy are no longer together, and that crystal is going to hurt me.*

Yes, he was feeling like he was bad and had done something wrong, because Mommy and Daddy were no longer together. He believed that he was the *bad* reason. Hmmm. . . .. my heart was quite sad knowing this.

I took his hand and assured him that he was good. I assured him he was loving, and I put the crystal in his hand. He didn't want to hold. I could see in his struggle to get away that he was worried he was going to be burned, but I held firm to his hand. I knew the gift that was to come.

I said in the softest voice I could, "Ryan, listen to me. Feel that; feel the love in the crystal. It doesn't want to harm you; it only wants to help and heal you. Can you feel its love?" I kept telling him over and over to feel the love. I said to him, "Close your eyes and trust me." For this little guy, that was a miracle in itself to trust me, some new and perfect stranger. But you know what? Love knows love, and he trusted me. He closed his eyes and listened as I told him to let the crystal act like a sponge. I told him to embrace it with both arms, hold it close to his heart, and let it suck out all of the pain and sadness his heart, all the pain he was feeling.

It was so beautiful to watch that not only was he listening and doing it, but his stepdad's eyes were now leaking from tears as he watched this little boy who would rather not listen to anyone anymore, listen.

He was listening. I said to him, "Hold it close to your heart for a few minutes, and when the crystal has done its job, you will feel joy inside." I let him stand there, all the while urging him to do what he was doing. I knew it would help. It wasn't quite two minutes when all of a sudden this huge smile was on his sweet face.

He gave me a grin as he opened his eyes. "I feel better now," he said. Wow, wow, *wow!* Not only was he feeling better, but so was *I,* knowing the power of something that not everyone can see or understand had taken place. Within moments, he was off and running about outside. His stepdad and I were in awe of the blessing we had just witnessed.

Later that day the guests were off to their designated rooms. Stepdad, Mom, and kids were off to the rose room—our lovely pink room that had been set up with crystals and prayers for tragedies of the heart. I knew they all needed that room. Grandma and Grandpa were off to sleep in the amethyst room—a room made for peace, tranquility, and protection but most of all for healing energy. I knew the grandparents needed a peaceful rest.

The next day came, and I awoke to laughter and people talking and scurrying around so as to continue on with their journeys. I had told them all that they would have an awesome night's rest and that healing spirit doctors visit the rooms, so enjoy the stay. They all wanted me to know how wonderful a night's rest they had and how peaceful, safe, restful, and healing the rooms' energies felt.

Blessed be and thanks to spirit. All was as it should be—perfect in our home and perfect in the universe. Before they all left, I gave out crystals to almost all, except for two of the babes whom I didn't want eating their crystals. I gave protection crystals to Mom and Dad, love crystals to Grandma and Grandpa, and a rose quartz crystal to Ryan. I told Ryan to carry it with him and when he felt sad to hold it near his heart, close his eyes, and to meditate like I had shown him. That way, he could release his sadness and pain if he needed to. He smiled and thanked me.

I was ecstatic inside to have touched, with my wife, such loving and wonderful souls. It would be about two days later when I heard from Mom and Dad who let me know that one night they were worried Ryan may have lost his crystal. They told me that they had gotten him ready for bed, and when they checked his clothes for the crystal, it was gone and they panicked that he had lost it. They were concerned, because they knew it had been helping him. Soooooo they went to his room and asked him if he had the crystal. And he gave them the most precious response back. He told them, "Oh, I already put it next to my bed so that when I wake up in the morning, it will be the first thing I see." I can only tell you about the tears in my eyes at this very moment, as I write this. *That* was priceless. I love the innocence and purity of a child.

Do your best, parents, to help preserve that. I still know my life was what it was. I know I learned to love because of the family I chose to be with. What are you learning with your choices?

I am going to send that little boy a desire he has. He had a wish, and he wanted a diamond. I found out that it wasn't a diamond he had wanted but a clear quartz crystal like I carry in my front pockets. He felt mine were magical, and he was hoping that maybe he could get one. I guess his wish will come true.

Strange how darkness came to me in the shape of a very angry human being who only wanted to stop me from doing what I needed to do—love. Darkness wanted a storm to come and ensure that these guests couldn't arrive and stay at our Healing Bridge, our home. Will all believe this story? I can only hope so. I know it happened. But then truly, I honestly don't care who believes this, as I and my wife, my son lived it. We were blessed and were made stronger for it. Our wings grew much larger because of it.

So always remember that even though storms come, you are the light of the world, so lighten up the world already. Who knows who will be able to see a brighter light, just because of you.

Oh, and a by the way, earlier in the story, it was most incredible to know that another electrical truck (in addition to the many that had already came) stopped at our home to ask us if we had power. When we said yes, they were surprised to hear we had power. The last man stopped by twice, and on the last stop, he wanted my wife to know that we were one of the lucky ones to actually get our power back. Most of our neighbors didn't have any power as of yet, and they didn't know when they would be getting power. Again, this was three days after the storm.

Thanks, Dad, for yelling at me to stay. Thanks, grandmas and grandpas and aunts and uncles and family and friends, who have crossed over to spirit and gone home while rooting for me to do what needs to be done—continue to be loving and peaceful and raise vibrations every day. I always say thanks to Elia for always believing in me. She has witnessed firsthand the powers of the universe in the seen and the unseen with me.

I said to someone along life's journey, "When you don't think that spiritual things exist, remember this: you can't see the message floating in the air when you use your cell phone, can you? Well, it's the same with spirit. Just because you can't see spirits existence doesn't mean that higher energies and lower energies and/or dark energies don't exist."

I do my best not to give low energies the time of day, but when they decide to tread in my space, where they don't belong… I spread love and my soul's light. I raise my vibrations high, so if anything wishes to be stop me from doing what I know I have to do, then they will have to raise in consciousness to be with me. I guess for me it's that I think one day maybe that person will also raise their consciousness to a level of peace, love, and spiritual enlightenment. I will be a spiritual soldier for the universe with all the rest of the light workers doing their jobs, raising consciousness for all.

"Life changes because of
the power called you!"

Love,
Emmanuel

THE LETTER

For some time, my wife had wanted to see Sylvia Browne for a psychic reading. She loves Sylvia and has all of her books. Unfortunately, my sweet Elia was never, at least as of this moment, able to have a private reading with Sylvia.

One day we received this little card in the mail with an advertisement for James Van Praagh. After reading it, my Elia said to me, "Look, Emmanuel! James Van Praagh is going to be in New York City."

I smiled to her saying, "Wow, are we doing anything at that time? Maybe we can go and see him."

Elia went on to tell me that it was going to be a weekend training for mediumship. "Right up our ally," I said to her. "Let's see if we can book the day and go." So, we booked the date and were soooooo excited.

I'd heard of James and had some of his books, but I'd actually never read any of them. The time had come to read his books.

I became in awe of what James had done for so many with his beautiful gift to talk with spirits that had crossed over. Elia and I had done medium work but were nowhere near as talented as James. I decided that I was going to start a manifesting meditation. I decided that if I were to go to see James, I was going to do my very best to manifest my dad to come through James and have a chat with me.

I and Elia would begin our day with our manifesting meditation and end the day on the same note, asking Dad to find his way to me at the New York City weekend. I was determined. I remember saying, "You didn't do much for me in life, so do this one thing for me, Dad, just this one thing. Show up, because now I know you know how much I have *always* loved you."

I and Elia continued to meditate right up to the day we were finally able to go and have our lives change forever—for the better. Dad even showed up just before we left while I was painting a mural on my home's ceiling. My Elia was sitting on our couch, while I was on the high stepladder painting the ceiling. She told me how my dad was watching me and described to me how he looked. She was so right; that was my dad. He wanted me to know that he was sorry he didn't understand what my art had meant to me while he was physically alive. I felt his presence but didn't get to see him as Elia did that day. But Dad did show up, and I thank him every day now for showing up and healing my life as I know it. Never pass the chance to say I love you. *Never!*

This is a letter my dad asked me to write after the workshop in New York City. I sent it to many per his request and I kept it true to his message and the purpose it had. I believe he wishes it to continue, so be blessed by its love. My life was what it was—no blame, just words of truth. I love my family and always will. I love my dad and am blessed to know that even beyond the grave, love still flows abundantly.

Dear Roberta,

Thank you so much for always writing to me. I apologize for not writing sooner. First, to address your letter and package of family tree items. The letters from my dad were an amazing gift. I will have to explain more in a moment, however, thank you for sending, all, that you have sent. So sorry to hear about Barbara, yet I know all is well and as it should be in the universe. I have always felt that there are no mistakes in life, just lessons to learn and moments to learn and grow by, even as painful as some seem.

Unfortunately, I am not in contact with any of the family except for you. I look at that as a gift and blessing, yet I know that soon all things in my life are going to get even better and change. I looked at the letters that you had sent of my dad's and just smiled remembering how much I loved my dad. I hadn't talked with him for about 12-13 years, there was a few brief moments, and then he died.

I can remember the last time I saw him in the physical sense, I held his face and said, "I want you to know how much I love you, Dad, I don't think I will be seeing you again." He told me of course they (my parents) were going to talk again; he would seem me next week or so.) That day never came. I knew better, as they always wanted me to be **In their life instead of being in mine.**

I didn't mourn, because I knew that he was in a much better place. As an adult, I always felt that death is actually life and that life is more like death. Life is more a hell of a sort. (Hope you got a smile at that one). I have had 3 near-death experiences, which helped to keep me focused on my journey.

As a child, I used to have visions and see things that most others did not visually see. In my home growing up, I had to ask my visions to go away. The Christian church my parents attended taught against that, so rather than go against the church and my family's beliefs, I asked them to go away. I am grateful most stayed.

I remember telling my mother that we are all earth Angels. She couldn't believe that, as it went against her church's beliefs. I shut my mouth until I, as an adult, got cancer, and it happened to be a tumor next to my throat in the left side of my neck. Why am I telling you all of this? You will see in a moment more.

My dad once told me how he was so disappointed that I had done nothing with my life. I remember saying, "I think six beautiful children is an amazing accomplishment." Many times my dad would tell me over and over how I should let go and just put up with my brothers' and sisters' crap. They all, as older siblings, thought they should always cast their "shit" on me.

I would speak to my parents and even my wife at the time, and they would say, "Oh, just let it go. I am sure it's nothing." It was always something painful physically or mentally. I knew I would one day have to make a choice, or all the crap from the family was going to physically break me down until I got another cancer and then finally die. I had to find a place that I could just be me without being harassed by my family every second of every day!

Once again, I went to my parents and asked for just a bit of their support, and they decided that it was best to trust the others and not me. My wife and I seemed to become more distant, as she wanted me to shut up and just get along with whatever. So ... no support from my parents for my life and no support from my wife for our life together, a continual up hill battle. But blessed be, I always did have my inner strength.

I remember many years ago when we were all at a Pudgies Pizza in Watkins Glen, my siblings were laughing and having a good time at my expense, and my parents just sat and listened. I remember them say to my parents, "Hey, remember when we were kids and we said he had lied and did this or took that? Well, guess what. We actually lied just to get him in trouble."

I heard, "Remember when he would have a birthday, and his stuff would turn up missing the next day? Well, we stole it and sold it in school and got money for all his stuff we stole. Remember all of those spankings he got because of what we said he did? Well, he didn't do it.. . ."

. . . . I remember looking at my mother, and she said to me, "I am so sorry. I didn't know." I remember my exact words to her: "No, Mother, you are wrong. I told you every day. You just never listened; you never believed me"

There really is an amazing reason I am telling you this, and it is such an amazing blessing. I just need to share it with as many as will listen. So in summary, my parents never really supported the "Way I was," as they would say. I was told I dressed differently, acted differently, I wore earrings, and loved different colors in my hair and, and, and just loved being who I am.

In the same, I didn't have the support of my wife either. She wanted me normal. I was hearing quite often, "You shouldn't wear that," or "Why did you do that?" My wife at the time would even say to me, "Are you actually going to go out looking like that?"

I remember a sister-in- law saying when she first met me, "You're not anything like your brother told me. He said you were not a guy and not a girl; you were more like a freak." She told me those words, and I was just amazed why anyone who knew me would say such hurtful things, as I had always loved them. But you and I both know as well as many others on this planet, hurtful ignorant words are unfortunately slung about every day, and sadly enough, hurtful words do actually hurt.

One of the last times I and my parents spoke was when I had had just about enough of all the arguing and bickering and taunting, and my mother was in one of her moods. I walked into the sawmill and spoke to my dad. I was asking and speaking to him about the family and my mother and asking if he could say something to get them to just leave me alone. He basically told me he could not and wasn't going to get involved, and I should just listen to them and just get along without causing anymore problems. I remember my wife agreeing.

I remember saying, "Dad, you don't get it. I am not the one causing the problems." With that said, I again said to my dad, "Would you please speak to my mother."

He stopped what he was doing and said in a very angry voice, "I am not going to say anything. _You_ don't understand. I have to live with that woman."

With that said, I left the building and went to where my mother was sitting in the vehicle reading and brooding. She rolled down the window a bit, and I began to do my best to express to her my concerns and wishes for her, for the family members, the neighbor (my brother). She snapped at me, and I replied back "Mother . . . Grow up!" She stopped talking to me that day. Who was I to tell her to grow up?

So to catch up with the times, I separated myself from the family, and my health got better. Got a divorce, and my health got better. Fell in love and got married in Boston, and my health got better. Moved to Boston, and wow, my health got better. Not to say there weren't a few health issues, but life seemed to be getting better and better.

Then something very special happened. I started getting messages on one of my electronics. My iPad has a game in it called Bookworm. It's a game like scrabble that spells out words, but it gives you about fifty tiles in a framed area, and then you look for the words. I would touch the button, the fifty tiles would show up, and sentences would appear instead of words. It kept saying, "Dad, Don, I am Don, Dad's here."

I have taken many pictures of them the many times I have got messages. I thought, "How funny. My dad couldn't talk to me in life but is now talking to me in death." I then had people giving me spiritual messages from my dad. Then I get an envelope from my Aunt A in Florida of my dad. Then I get an envelope from you, Roberta, with letters of my dad's. Then I and my lovely wife Elia (sounds like Ee-Lee'-uh) paid for a weekend retreat with a world-renowned physic medium named James Van Praagh. He helped write and produce "The Ghost Whisperer," a TV show. I kept asking that if my dad were actually sending me messages that James would pick me if he decided to read the class of a few hundred.

It was the second day in New York City. We were at the seminar, and we had just got back from lunch when James said, "I think we will now have a demonstration." I felt this incredible pull in my gut towards the stage and felt my dad. All of a sudden James says, "I have this older gentleman here with me in his late seventies-ish when he crossed over. He says he goes by the name Ron, Ronnie, Ronald. Does that sound familiar to anyone?"

I was crying so hard that my wife had to raise her hand for me. She told James, "That's my husband's dad; his name was Don, Donnie, Donald."

There was quite a gasp in the audience. I was already crying so hard it was hard for me to breathe. I knew I felt my dad. I knew my dad was here with me. James told the helper to bring me the microphone as James continued with, "He has rosy cheeks like someone put rosy dots on his cheeks. One on each cheek." He said to me, "Is this correct?"

I said, "Yes, that's my dad."

James said, "I see he is wearing blue jeans like bib overalls, coveralls, and a white T-shirt." James said, "Your dad is telling me that you have a picture of him in his T-shirt and overalls. Is that true?" I told him yes. James said, "He is balding on top. He said he has a bigger chest, and in life he was a strong man." James said, "He is telling me when he was in the hospital and when he was there, they put something in his throat, and he didn't like it as it bothered his throat." James said, "Is this true?"

I told him that I didn't know, as my family didn't talk with me. James said, "Well, keep that information, as someone else in your family will know, and that will be a message to them that he is fine."

With tears flowing like a waterfall, I said, "I will do that."

James said, "He crossed over because of his heart. Did he die of a heart attack?" Again, I told James I didn't know, as my family didn't talk so I knew to just keep the information documented.

James then told me, "He is telling me that he lived in a country rural setting on a farm that had a barn and silos." James asked if this were true, and I said yes. James said, "Your dad is telling me that he used to attend a church in life. Is that so?" I said yes.

The audience just listened in awe at the connection that was given to me by way of Spirit. James continued and said, "Your dad wants you to know that he is here with Robert." James asked if I knew who Robert was, and I was not able to recall but documented it for later. I knew a few Roberts in spirit.

James said, "Your father is telling me that he is connected to a woman who was from the Midwestern states, and you are connected to her as well." James then said, "Do you know whom he is referring to?"

I said, "Yes, that would be my mother."

"He is saying your mother is stuck in her book."

I shook my head, knowing what book. A black book with gold trim—I knew what he meant and acknowledged it to James to let my dad know I understood. Each and every moment, gasps were made in the audience by the information that was being shared and by the tears that I was shedding in waterfalls of joy in knowing my dad had made a very special journey to speak with me.

James then said, "He is showing me someone that is living near the Ohio region. Would you know of this?"

I shook my head no. Through the tears, I said, "At the moment, I am not sure."

Then James said, "Your father is showing me that your family is in discourse, disconnected; they don't talk to you." James said, "Is that correct?"

I said, "Yes, that's true."

James said, "Your dad wants to acknowledge that and says that he is sorry. He wants to apologize to you and say he is so sorry that he didn't know in life and he didn't understand and now he does, and he wants you to know that he is sorry." James said, "Do you understand?"

I said yes with a waterfall of tears flowing.

James then said, "Your dad wants you to know that he is proud of you, of how free you are to be who you are." Then James started saying, "Damn, damn, DAM You gotta stop it." James said, "Your dad is kind of doing this little shaking thing saying 'damn, damn, dam , you. You gotta stop it. You've gotta stop being so hard on yourself. You're too hard on yourself.'" James looked at me and said, "Is this true?"

I said, "Yes."

James said, "Well, maybe you should listen to your dad and stop being so hard on yourself."

I agreed. I was and am way too hard on myself, and I would do my best to forgive myself and move on.

James then said, "Your dad is telling me that you are connected to two other males. You have two other brothers and that you have been separate for a long time. Is that so?"

I said, "Yes."

James said, "Well, your father wants me to tell you that he understands that you are disconnected from your brothers and that as for your brothers are concerned, you are much better than them." James said, "Do you understand that?"

With the waterfall of tears still flowing, I said yes and shook my head as such. James then said , "Your dad is showing me the name of Tex and says, 'Tell him that Tex is with me.'" James said, "Do you know a Tex?" And I said No. He said, "Well, your father is spelling it out in bold, capital letters: T-E-X." James said to just document it for a later time and maybe I would find out who Tex is "because your dad is telling me it is important for you to know that Tex is with him."

James then said, "He is showing me that you have someone directly connected to you that lives in Florida. Is that true?"

I said, "Yes, my oldest son Caleb lives in Florida."

James said, "Well, your father wants me to tell you that Caleb is a healing tool for you." James said, "Do you know of a place in Florida called St. Lucie, St. Lucy?" I said no. He said, "Well, your father is telling me to urge you to go there. It's very good for you to go there to heal." James said, "Do you understand? Your dad is urging you to go there."

I said, "Yes, I will go there as soon as I can."

James said, "Your dad wants you to know that he likes your tattoos." James said to me, "Do you have tattoos?" He said, "Your dad says you do." I said yes. James said, "Yes, your dad is telling me that you do, and he likes the three winged ones. He says that you have three that are alike." James said, "Does this make sense to you?"

I said, "Yes, I have three colorful butterflies on my chest, and they are exactly alike."

James said, "Yes, your dad is telling me he loves the butterflies. He loves their color. Yes, it's the butterflies." James then said, "Your dad is telling me something about a car, about a car being a gift." James said, "Did your dad give you a gift in the form of a car? He is telling me about a car being a gift."

And through an ocean of tears, I told him, "No, I gave my dad a car." ... ... I do believe most in the audience were crying with me as James said, "Yes, that's it. Your dad is acknowledging that _you_ gave him a car and is telling me to thank you. He just wants to acknowledge and thank you for that. He didn't get to do that in life, and he wants to thank you."

This went on for a bit over fifteen minutes, and then as fast and powerfully felt as my dad came, James said, "Well, before your dad goes, he wants you to know that he is with you more now than before and can now help you more than he ever could, and he wants you to know that he ... loves you!"

I am forever changed, and a healing has been taking place ever since. I have lived through burns, cancer, ulcers, a stroke, a leg filled with blood clots, psoriasis with its raw spots inflamed and itching continually, broken bones from childhood, broken bones from adulthood, fingers cut off, feet nailed to a two-by-four, a sledgehammer axe catapulted at the center of my chest while time stood still for an angel to save me from death. And, unfortunately, the list can go on for a few pages but after a gift of "forgive me" from my dad, I now know truth—his "I love you." Healing begins in a most amazing way.

I know I am changed by this moment forever. I have always known there was no hell, but the hell we all put each other through here on Earth. Now after talking with my father, I know it's okay to be me and not beat myself up for being me anymore. It's okay to like whatever hair I choose, wear my earrings, tattoos, and even my bib overalls to the Ming Theater to watch a Broadway performance. It's okay and great to be me!

I know you loved your dad and miss him often. I know he is with you always, smiling and whispering in your ear occasionally, so just listen with your heart and know he loves you always.

I hope this letter and story has helped you in some way. I know I have shed many tears in just writing it, as every time I think of my dad's visit and the love he sent and gave me at the Omega convention in New York City with James Van Praagh, I shed some more tears. Not tears of sadness, though. Tears of a love that I know is eternal and nonjudgmental. Tears that are healing to me every moment of every day and just loving from my dad.

I have always loved my dad, and now I know he knows that. Just to let you know, the psoriasis is almost gone since my dad's visit—just a few small pink spots that are almost completely gone. So far, blood clots are gone, got my broken nose fixed, and had to have my crushed nasal cavity rebuilt; however, my life is awesome.

So with that, I will say, once again, ... Thank you for writing and sharing. Not writing and judging and arguing bickering and complaining that I am not what you want me to be. But, yep, one more time: thank you for just writing and chatting to just share.

> With a Great Love,
> Emmanuel

I am much freer as my dad knows to be me. .... and the best part is we can change our names, we can even change our sex if we choose, we can change and choose anything we want because life is our very own to choose and make choices for. Not anyone else's but our very own. I choose for only me. I choose yes!

P.S.: Since leaving the past behind, I have been to England, Greece, Egypt, Italy, Venice, Croatia, Turkey, Santorini, The Bahamas, St. Thomas, St. Barts, Dominican Republic, am now a certified scuba diver along with my wife, and we have both also been skydiving. Life is too short not to experience it. We will be spending another two weeks at two more seminars this year learning to hear spirit and become better mediums, as to help others as we have been helped. One week will be with just James Van Praagh, and the other week will be with James and four other psychic mediums from around the world. We will be traveling soon to Florida to see what my dad wanted me to see and feel in Florida, besides seeing Caleb. We will be traveling to Arizona for two weeks' rest and healing time.

But, however, at the present time, I am here in Boston. I hardly ever return to New York home, as each time we do, the neighbor tends to find out we are there and does his best to harass us. I choose peace not to be in pieces. But I am learning new ways to move on and not be bothered by the past, as yesterday is no longer here unless I bring it with me.

A few weeks ago my wife's mom died, and she went back to her town alone but stopped by the home in New York to look for a few personal items left behind. Unfortunately, neighbors found out someone had driven up to our home, and he proceeded to drive their four-wheeler up in the woods and yell over the fence, taunting my wife. They are sad people whom I am blessed to no longer have in my life but will choose to send them love.

__The letter and story I wrote was not one of complaints and woes but just another story of someone's existence and their will to survive, rise above it, and just move on__. I wish all the best whether they be family or not. But as for the family ,I wish them the best, but without me. . . . My life is blessed, and I now finally "Live."

> "Live and be happy with what you have lived."
> Emmanuel

I almost forgot: I hadn't written also because I was attending college. I had to finish college and rest for a bit. Who would have thought at my age I would go back to school, leave college with a 4.0? . . . . . . Funny thing, I am thinking of going to another college to fulfill another lifetime dream of mine! Who knows, right? Be Blessed. I am!

KING AND BUTTERFLY

I was in the shower one day having inner dialogue with spirit about a butterfly. I heard butterflies are free to fly, and that is their purpose—to be beautiful and fly their rainbow of colors around for all to see. A butterfly seems to have no worries or cares; it just flies. Its dance seems to be so magical, as it always captures its watcher into a moment of trance. A butterfly comes in an assortment of colors, and no matter how much you want to train it, a butterfly has a mind of its own. You can't even pay a butterfly to do your wishes or to do your bidding for you. A butterfly is always bouncing and eating nectar and showing us all how carefree to be.

I once knew a beautiful maiden who said, "My nickname is Butterfly." My queen and I met her and heard her butterfly story of transformation and change and felt good in that moment with her presence. My queen said to me, "I wish I could visit with her again. I wish we could invite her to our castle for a visit."

So with love, I sent the butterfly some golden coins and said, "Butterfly, could you please come and visit us in our castle so far away? We will give you a resting place. We will give you the nectar you need to live. We will give you love."

Butterfly had a mind of her and said, "Hmm, dearest King, as loving as you are, I cannot carry the golden coins. They are too heavy, and I have no need for them in my life. My life in my land of sand castles is not like yours, and I like the flowers and the sand and sunshine. Yet someone else has trouble in their life. Let me see I think I will give the golden gift away. Someone else needs at least half the gift."

So Butterfly gave half the gift away and said, "I can't come and visit you my king, because I have to fly around my flowers. I have to spread my wings and let my color shine wherever today takes me. I need to drink the nectar in my own land to survive. I cannot leave my sun, my sand, and my flowers. I am sorry, dearest King. I cannot come to your land to visit you."

My day turned sad as I walked the path of my kingdom. I looked around my kingdom, and all I could see was its beauty. I needed to realize there was a message that each of us has a choice, and that is to be respected. A great king knows truth and the greatness in living one's truth. I smiled and looked down to the ground and saw this beautiful creation. Its life was almost over. It seemed to have such a short life, as I had only seen it a day or so ago, on my path's walk.

It was a butterfly. I knew that in the kingdom I lived there were also butterflies of a vast beauty. I knew their journey was flying here and there, yet I also knew that one must just embrace what they have, as within a moment's notice, their life span is over like the butterfly.

Yes, I thought, *for the butterfly, the moment of life is here and then gone so fast, as in an instant.* I reached down and picked up the beautiful butterfly and gave it love as I watched this amazing creation die in my hand. I took a moment to show thanks that I had been so blessed to have known this great creation of my vast kingdom. I was blessed to have known that it was free to be what it chose to be, something without judgment of self or others but simply beautiful.

I took the butterfly back to my kingdom and cased it in a beautiful vessel so I would always be able to enjoy its beauty and remember the moment it helped me gain more wealth in wisdom. The butterfly in life helped make my kingdom a brighter place and in its death still left me the colors of its love to see always. Now I would begin a new adventure.

I knew that I wished the butterfly could have known me, but that was not the butterfly's purpose, to fulfill my heart's desire. Its purpose was to be free to fly and be true to itself. The new journey for me was now to be forever free too. Free to be me, happy with my own path. Yes, I knew my path was a different one, and it wasn't one of flying free and yet, was it?

Whatever you are, know you are perfect no matter what you are. Know in the essence of life, you have been so magically placed in the position of learning that which you have chosen. Know that if it is your job in life to fly, then fly and fly the best you can. If it is your position in life to sit, then be the best sitter you can. If it's your job to pray, then be the best prayer you can. If it's your job to be a teacher of love, life, math, history, music, spirit, then do your best without judgment to be the best you can be and just be that. Don't look around to see who's looking; just be the best you can be. I know I am not a butterfly; I know I am a king. I know I must and will continue to be free, but be free to be me.

I learned a lot that day, that day in the shower. I washed away yesterday and moved into a new moment of awareness; I became aware that my agenda is mine and —no one else's. My life and its lessons are about me, and if I am being loving and true to me, I am always being true to you.

Be what you are
meant to be.

Love,
Emmanuel

THANKS, MARTHA.

Many years ago as a child, I can remember visiting some of my mother's family in Wichita, Kansas. We went with the family to their church. I will never forget the service as long as I live. It was join-the-church day. There were about a hundred people there, and they were all white but one woman. I paid no mind, because as a child, I always felt that all were the same—beautiful souls with a life experience.

It was time for the service to begin, and the minister said, "Before we begin the service today, we need to have a congregational vote. We have someone here who has been attending our services for some time now, and we all know who she is. Well, Martha wants to join our congregation and become a member, so I think we all need to vote at this time."

I remember thinking, *Who is Martha?*

The minister then instructed, "Martha, would you please stand up before the congregation so we can vote on whether you can become a member or not of our church?"

Martha stood up, and there standing now was this absolutely beautiful black woman. She looked like everybody's grandma. I fell in love with her immediately. I just wanted to run over and squeeze her and ask her if she would be mine. She was wearing a lovely black and purple flowered dress. Her hair looked like she had just left the beauty parlor, and she had on this stunning hat with a tiny veil. She was obviously dressed for an occasion, and now I knew what she was dressed up for.

It wasn't just for church; it was for the special occasion of joining a church, becoming part of something larger than what she thought she already was.

The minister made it so businesslike, having someone open the meeting and then calling it all to order. Then he said, "All right now, all who give a 'yay' for Martha; show a raise of hands."

What happened next took me by great surprise, as no one raised their hands for Martha. I was horrified. Here stood this beautiful human being only wanting to be part of a church as a member, and because of her color, she was told by a show of hands *no*.

Next, the minister said, "Now a show of hands for 'nay.'" The entire congregation raised their hands to publicly say no to Martha.

Martha had been publicly humiliated. I was so ashamed to be sitting in such an awful place. Martha stood there with such grace while the church she loved said no to her. To me, Martha was much greater than what she had hoped to be part of. Martha was greatness to me that day.

The minister said, "I am sorry, Martha, but we can't be having your kind join our churches, or we will be having many bombings in our churches. I am so sorry." And with that, he went on to preach his sermon.

I felt so dirty and devastated that I would hear anyone, *especially* a minister, say those words out loud to another human soul. I couldn't wait to leave. My eyes still fill with tears for Martha. I can say that my dad and mom at that time and my brothers and sisters were all horrified as well. She only wanted to become part of something bigger, like the family the church represents, She wanted to be part of what the church calls the "Body of Christ." However, she didn't know rejection was waiting for her because she wasn't the color *they* wanted— and that color was white; *only* white.

I do hope Martha found a much better place to worship. Though many years have passed and my life has changed in so many ways, bigotry is unfortunately still as rampant as ever. I know so many gay couples who are now being so harshly judged and are being told by so many upstanding good citizens that they are second-rate and that they cannot marry because only a marriage between a man and a woman is constitutional. Such crap—it is not *constitutional*; it is *personal choice*. And when gays are shunned and told they cannot have the same rights as all of the rest., it is as shameful as the way people treated Martha.

So many tell me how much they love me and how much respect they have for me, and yet they want to keep I and my beautiful wife as second-class as Martha was treated. A few years back I married the most wonderful man in the world because of love. He said, "You do know I am transgender."

I remember saying, "I don't care what you are, because all I know is that I am in love with *you*."

We had been married awhile, and then my beautiful husband said, "I need to be the woman that lives in side."

I remember saying, "I support you, because I love you, and that is that. I love *you*."

He went through all of what he needed to do and became the beautiful woman she is now. There was no fear, because it was about loving self, not judgments of others. We love each other and did what came naturally; we let who we are shine.

I have read many articles about "gay marriage" and all I can say to those who are using the term "gay marriage," you know nothing of what you say. Marriage is marriage, and that is that. Love is not a color or a race; it is the perfection of how and what we are in the human existence.

I was married to a woman for many years, and we had six children together. I was married to a man and lived in heaven even without the rights that so many others have. I now live with my beautiful transgender wife and still live in heaven, but still have the same limited rights as when I was married to a man, because the government does not acknowledge that we have rights as "heterosexual couples." Shame on the self-righteous who still treat all human beings like Martha was treated. Love knows no boundaries; love only knows love. So if you treat others without love, then you don't know love at all.

Today I write this because someone sent me a political add to support someone who is against gay issues and freedom for all. They wanted me to support cutting off part of the human race because they loved differently than others. Again, love is love, but judgment is judgment.

Recently, I watched an interview with a man and a presidential candidate. This beautiful gay veteran wanted to know if the candidate would support him and his husband. The candidate said he would only support marriage between a man and a woman. My heart ached for the veteran. He only wanted to look after and care for his spouse—the one he loved and was married to.

Voting seasons can and usually are so filled with righteous cruelty. Please remember: voting is an awesome personal choice. We all have the right here in America to have that privilege. Please try to remember that loving someone with all of your heart and soul is also a personal choice. One should not be killed because of that beautiful choice called *love*.

The other day my daughter was telling me how her best friend was taking a history course on religion. While taking this history of religion course, she was the only one in the classroom who had a different opinion on religion: all were Christians but her. They made her feel like Martha and they laughed at her for not having the same opinion as theirs. She said the professor even paid no mind as they all enjoyed that she was the brunt of the joke. How sad in this day and age, the truth of Martha's story resoundingly rings. My heart went out for Kennedy. I know how it feels to be the only one in the room all the while you're being made fun of standing up for what you believe is your truth. It takes courage to stand up for your truth, but it doesn't take courage to be a bully. Live your truth, not mine. I honor all of the Kennedys and all of the Marthas and all the gays, lesbians, bi's, transgenders and to all of those who are a little different than the "norm"; all of those who stand up for the truth, even when it comes with a cost of being ostracized by the group.

When are we going to grow and see that we are all different, and we can all get along? This change begins with you and is passed on by you. I ask you for nothing. I give you truth. What is your truth? Is it loving to all or to just a few? Can you not see that although a tree is different, it likes hugs too? Imagine if we all were able to walk around hugging and loving each other, everywhere, every day. You *know* the world would be such a better place!

I say for me, I will always open my heart and mind, so you can have total freedom. I will ask spirit to help you open your hearts as well to see bigotry and segregation are not special groups that we should belong to. Loving thy neighbors and treating all with dignity and kindness is a group we should all aspire to be part of.

I remember saying to someone, "If you choose to send me any info that says vote for someone who wants to keep me and 'my kind' from having freedoms and rights too—the same ones that you have—know that I will exercise my own right and toss the info away."

Martha, I know you are in spirit now. I hope you had an amazing life and found love wherever you went. If you are listening or reading this as I write, please know you were and are an amazing inspiration of love to me. You helped teach me that it didn't matter the color of one's skin, race, or sexuality. You showed me life was filled with a rainbow. You just wanted to be part of something that you thought was better. I hope in life you found it.

I recently walked into a "spiritual" store in our area. This woman working there said to I and Elia, "Oh look, the *gays* are here! I just love it when the *gays* come and visit us!"

I will tell you, my eyes were very opened at that moment. I was a bit surprised to hear her say those words to us. One of our safe havens had just become a place of ridicule and judgment. I did have a chat with this woman. She laughed and thought she was hysterical. I wasn't laughing. She needed to have walked in Martha's shoes—in the shoes of love. Love will laugh *with* you   not *at* you.

I have always wished that people could understand such a simple thing. We are not a race, we are not a color, we are not a cliquey little group. We are soul—all of us beautiful, perfect souls on a journey called life. We are no different from each other, just souls here on a class trip called the human experience. Do your best to share your toys no matter what age. Love and be loved.

Always loving you the best I can,
Love Emmanuel

Be someone's
Inspiration today.

Love,
Emmanuel

CHOPPING WOOD
IN THE CRICK

I will never forget hearing my e-mail give that little ding to let me know that mail had just arrived in my box. I opened the computer and checked my mail only to see and read the following: "Padre, make sure you write a story about the sledgehammer axe down in the crick." Yes… that was quite a day. That was another day when I could have died, but God, Mother God, Angels, guardians, guides, spirit, everything in the universe was watching over me. My life was made another miracle that day.

It was wintertime, and we heated our home with wood. I had been living using wood heat since I can't remember when. Growing up in the country on an extremely poor farm, we cut wood all the time during the winter months so as to keep the fires burning. As a child, I can remember feeling half frozen to death and wishing I was back in the home with that warm heat instead of being in the freezing cold woods cutting up and carrying wood. Funny, how as a child we at times think that the wood will just magically appear, and all will be well.

That didn't happen to be the case, though; we had to travel up on our hill, riding on a wagon pulled by our dad's tractor. Sometimes the wind would be blowing a fury, but that never stopped us. Without the wood in the cellar, the home would become an instant refrigerator. I knew that we would have to cut wood, load it, then unload it, carry it, and stack it in the cellar of our home—the dungeon, as my mother called it.

So what does this have to do with the story that my son wanted to make sure that I wrote? A lot. But most of all, it's a good memory of something much greater than me watching over me, so I could see another day. But even more, it's to show my son that we are never alone and a much greater power truly exists.

You see, to a child, cutting wood in the winter may have been a nightmare, but cutting wood to an adult like my dad, was a magical moment in time. As an adult, I am able to understand that. We as parents do what we can, and let's say a lot of us do the best we can, even when our children think we are doing the worst for them. And when we grow up and become adults ourselves, we are able to see that our parents didn't come with a book of guidelines; they came with themselves and then did the best they could to teach us with their life's training. So now on to the crick, which I grew up always calling a *crick*—yes, not a creek.

It was around the year 2005, and it was very cold. Wintertime was upon us, and it was time to make sure we had plenty of wood cut for the winter months. I had noticed that down near the crick one of the trees was dying,, and it needed to come down before it hurt someone. So off I went with my son Aubrey, my chainsaw, and tools to get the job done. What a blessing that Aubrey was there with me that day, as without him there, this story would never have been believed.

The tree was about two and a half feet in diameter, and it took a bit of time to cut down. I fell the tree and started cutting it up in chunk lengths so that when I was finished, I would be able to take my axe and chop it all up into pieces that would fit into the wood stove. Some of the wood chunks that I cut rolled down the embankment and into the water in the crick. That wouldn't be a problem to go into the crick and retrieve them, as I loved being out in the cool air, especially cutting wood. It really gave me good memories of my dad, and at that moment, one of my sons was with me making his own memories of being in the cool air cutting wood with his dad. The memories I had of cutting wood with my father really warmed my heart. Not that I liked it then, mind you, but I was no longer a child. I liked that, and I know I was smiling about it that day.

Well, the tree was so big that some of it had fallen across the crick, and was over the top of the bank on the other side. It had fallen on top of a town road that ran parallel to the crick. I would have to do a lot of quick cleaning up. Aubrey and I hurried over to cut the tree parts into chunks and rolled them to the side of the road so we could get it all out of the way of any countryside traffic that would be traveling up the road. We finished up and went back to the original side where we were cutting and worked about the day till we had finished there.

Many large chunks of the tree trunk had rolled down into the crick bed and were now resting in ice water. I wanted to get the chunks out of the water and put them in piles to eventually take to our home, which was at the top of a hill between five and six hundred feet away. But first, it was time to chop the wood that had landed on dry ground. I loved chopping wood with my axe and had a passion for it.

For many years my children had watched me cut wood chunks with my axe with the most amazing excitement, because every time I cut with my axe, it always seemed to be quite a magical moment. My childhood and family theme was survival of the fittest. I was a very strong young man and have maintained that even to this day—even now as a grandfather. As a child, I always loved cutting wood with the axe. Even though I know my dad didn't want me to touch an axe as a child, I also know he realized that I really, really enjoyed that experience.

So, I lifted the axe, and Aubrey watched: the magic was about to begin. Now before I go too far, I need to let you know that my axe was not just a plain old axe; it was a plastic, fiber-handled, sledgehammer axe. This sucker was big and heavy duty. It was a beast in weight, but I loved it and could swing it all day long, thanks to my childhood survival training. Picture this: you see my Aubrey now standing at a distance, waiting for the show to begin, and the sledgehammer falls. I started chopping as these massive chunks were exploding apart.

I would lift the axe and swing it down with a mighty force of power. It thrilled me, myself to watch the wood chunks explode with such a force that they would fly several feet away. I would finish up one area, and Aubrey would stack a big pile so we could get it all carried to the home later—hopefully, with help. Cutting wood was always a performance of great pleasure for me.

Now hours later, it was time to go down into the crick bed and get the chunks cut that were resting and floating in the water. I decided that instead of carrying up these massive chunks, I would just chop them in the crick on some flat stones and then carry up the pieces. That would make I and my son's lives much easier. So, I chopped up a storm, and when I had only a few chunks left, I said to my son, "I think I am going to go up on the other side of the crick and get those chunks by the road taken care of, so no one steals them overnight."

Unfortunately, we had people who would actually steal wood that I had stacked down by our crick bed. I was rather saddened that someone would steal the wood, knowing how hard I had worked for days to cut and stack it in order to keep my family warm.

I decided to cut by the road and remove easy temptation. Aubrey agreed. I left a few chunks stacked in the crick, went up near the road, and started chopping away. After a while, I realized there was so much tree to cut yet that I might have to continue another day. Again, my son agreed and we started throwing and carrying and stacking, but now we were having to carry it all twice as far. We were on the other side of the crick from our home, so in addition to the five hundred to six hundred feet from the house to the bank, it was fifteen to twenty feet down the steep bank to the crick, then about thirty feet or so across, and then fifteen feet up another steep bank to the wood on the road. The bank was slippery and mucky, the crick water was running like crazy, leaves were flying everywhere, and the crows in the trees wouldn't shut up. They had been yakking all day. Cars were flying up the road, so I knew I had to get that tree off of the road before someone said something.

The day was filled with life, and I was in heaven, not that my other children were happy and in heaven like me. They were the ones who didn't want to help me but needed to, so they were carrying the piled wood from our piles to the woodshed behind the home. What happened next would be only with I and Aubrey. We had our work totally cut out for us, but were in the groove and getting it all done. I decided that I needed to take my magical axe down into the crick so as not to forget it up by the road, or again someone would steal it... no thanks.

I slid down the bank and leaned the axe over a chunk of wood thinking nothing of it. I went back up the bank toward the roadside to bring back more tools and then throw more wood down into the crick bank. That would make it so much easier for I and my son, so we could carry it all up the other side.

Aubrey was taking wood up the bank that was near the home and piling it, but he continued watching me. Throughout my Aubrey's life, he has always seemed to be one of my guardian angels. He has always been there to catch me when I am falling. A room could be full of people, and he would be the only one to see I was in trouble. I had always called him Aubrey Joy because of the joy he brought to my life. There is never a dull moment with Aubrey.

I had no idea that I was going to be in big trouble very soon. Now Aubrey was on one side of the crick, and I was on the other. I was showing off at the moment and said, "Hey, Aubrey, check this out!" With my super strength, I was lifting up a very large chunk of oak tree. It was about twelve to fourteen inches in diameter and about thirty inches long. I told him, "Watch this," as I proceeded to throw it. I tossed it into the air, and instantly, the world as I knew it changed.

Within a split second, it was as if everything had stopped. Really. I mean *everything* was stopped like in super slow motion. I could see particles of wood shavings from my gloves holding still in the air, frozen in a moment of time. This huge chunk of wood was holding tight, motionless in the air. *Everything* in slow motion. Little did I know at that time, Aubrey was seeing exactly the same thing—again *everything* in slow motion. He was seeing the same wood particles and dust particles holding in midair, suspended in time. He was seeing the chunk of wood motionless in midair, but for what?

There was a silence that was so loud it was deafening. There had been a breeze blowing the leaves on the trees all around us, but now all the leaves were motionless and silent, as there was no longer wind blowing them. The trees were silent. The flowing water in the crick had stopped moving. I knew something was extremely wrong. We both felt something was wrong: no sound, no birds. Where were the loud crows that wouldn't shut up? There were no crickets, no nothing; everything was motionless and silent. I mean one moment there were birds singing, and now not a sound—only silence. As much as this moment was terrifying, it was just as awesome.

Oh my god am I that special that the world has just stopped for me?

"Yes," I heard. "Yes you are."

Within our next parallel moment, my son I saw what was about to happen. Aubrey would later tell me that he was also confused as to why things were moving so slowly, but when he looked down and looked into my eyes, he knew and saw there was trouble. We saw the chunk of wood I had thrown in the air heading straight down for the axe handle. Yet, we could see the chunk of wood barely moving. I mean, our bodies were frozen! We couldn't move; we could only process in our minds what was going on, and we were *both* intensely processing. It was a horror movie. We were stars in a show. Aubrey had the best seat in the house—unable to do anything but watch the events unfold. He was about to witness the death of his father.

Imagine throwing a handful of dirt in the air, and all of a sudden it stops and stays put. We remember feeling as if this was lasting an hour, and yet it happened in the blink of an eye.

Extremely slowly, time was actually moving as we were watching the wood fall but ever so slightly as if not to move at all. The strangest thing for I and Aubrey was when the wood finally hit the axe. We both knew it was going to hit it, we both knew the axe was going to come flying at me, but I don't think either of us ever in our wildest dreams would have expected what was happening to happen.

Aubrey and I could hear the sound of the axe cutting through the air as it flew back up toward me and pulsed through the air. There was a whooshing sound in a rhythm as it spun. Aubrey was seeing the same thing. I would only have a split second of reaction time, and I am so blessed for that. I was able to think, and think quickly.

I remember looking up in that split second that felt like minutes and seeing Aubrey having the same reaction as I was on the opposite side of the crick. He had just noticed in his moment of time that the immense size and weight of the oak chunk heading for the axe handle was really going to hurl that axe at me at quite a fast rate of speed. I can also remember Aubrey hearing my words in slow motion, "Holy shit!"

With the way I had placed the axe handle over another chunk of wood, that chunk of wood would act as a fulcrum. The handle was positioned in such a way that when the chunk from the air hit, the axe would hit me.

I and Aubrey both realize now, I was given this moment of time to allow me the way to go home or a split second of reaction time to stay. I knew I would only have that second to react, and my mind knew what it needed to do.

We both felt as if we were paralyzed as we could think but couldn't move. Remember, time was standing still for us, and we were in that moment of time. Just as time was very slowly starting to kick in for us both, I was able to begin lifting my arm to block the axe, although everything was still moving in slow motion. The axe was coming right at me, and I knew if I missed, the axe was going to kill me in front of my son. I knew it would be lights out for me, but it would be tragedy for Aubrey.

It's funny how we both knew and both could see that my life was going to end. I believe that in life we have checkpoints—points in life we can choose to go home by or continue on in life if we want to. For me, this was a checkpoint, but what would that mean for Aubrey?

Can you imagine being with someone you love and watching an axe split them open before your very eyes? That was not a moment I wanted Aubrey to bear. I knew I couldn't leave such a loving being with such tragedy to deal with. This was not going to happen. I was going to go on for yet another day. This moment in time was a gift for me, and I was going to choose life.

As my arm lifted almost to position, all went from slow motion to normal speed, and the axe flew. My arm hit the handle, and the handle hit me, stopping the blade from hitting me in the chest. The power and speed of the axe coming at me came with such a force that when it hit my arm, it turned the blade and the butt of the hammer. In the blink of an eye, it turned death to life, and the flat side of the cold steel hit me in the stomach. The butt of the axe slammed into me, and time kick-started.

The sheer force of the axe sent me hurling back two feet in the air and to the ground. I lay there in the gravel and sand on the edge of the road, gasping for breath with this sledge hammer axe now resting on top of me. It looked as if I had just laid down and placed the axe on my chest, and there we were.

Oh my god... I made it. I'm alive.

I can still feel the emotional impact as I write this. Crazy as it seems, I am shaking as I write and am chilled to the bone. That was another day I was shown by my universe that I was a living miracle. I was needed to be here for another day.

I can tell you, I have had to stop writing to wipe the tears from my eyes at this very moment. I will never and can never forget that day when time stood still for I and my son. Time stopped and gave me back to Aubrey. My life was spared because I *was* meant to write this story. I know God is there. I know there is a Father God, Mother God. I know there are angels and that we have guides and that there is only love, and I know I was needed and meant to be here today. My job on this planet is not yet over.

I will never forget Aubrey running over to me and screaming, "Oh my God, Padre!!! Are you *okay?!*" I could hear water splashing and leaves rustling as he ran over to me; birds chirping, and cars going by. I will never forget him saying, "Padre! The weirdest thing just happened! I saw everything in slow motion!"

In that same moment, I was trying to tell him, "Oh my God, Aubrey! Did you feel and see what just happened? Everything was in slow motion!"

I knew I was given that slow motion to have that single second of time to be able to react. Aubrey was thankful for that single second too. Thank you, God, Mother God, universe. Thank you, oneness. Thank you, angels. Thank you, guides. Thank you for giving me time and stopping time so that I am here today.

Although the sledgehammer hit me on the backside of my forearm and then in the stomach, lifting and setting me back two feet, I never had a bruise. It was red for a few hours and tender for a few days, but *never* did I bruise.

I know that over the years, Aubrey and I have remained close because of that moment. We shared something so unbelievable to most, but we know it happened. We lived it. I know that Aubrey was there just so he could see the miracle and *know* that there is *more* to life than just living. I know Aubrey was there to see that there is a force that watches over us all, and when it is our time to go home (die), then we go, and when it is not our time, all the powers of heaven make sure it doesn't happen. I do believe in miracles, and so does Aubrey. We were there, and we witnessed together the power of a higher existence making me a living miracle.

I *am* a miracle.

By the by... I still have my sledgehammer axe.

Look in the mirror
every day and always
tell who's looking
back you love them!

Love,
Emmanuel

MY NEW TAX ACCOUNTANT

So, I and my lovely Elia were off to the tax accountant office to get my taxes done. Joy, right?! We live in Boston, so rather than drive, we get to take the bus into town and then take the train into the city. I love the transit system in Boston. It always lets the kid in me come out to play. Anyhow, we rode in and got off the train to walk about a block to our destination. I love walking through the city, holding hands with the one I love, no matter if it is to go   to get   my taxes done.

We arrived at our destination only to see this lovely lady sitting at the front desk talking to two young people and filling in their information into the computer system. We stood at the counter for a few minutes before she said to us, "Is there someone I can get for you to see?"

I smiled, and my wife said, "Yes, we're here to see Addie."

The woman laughed and said, "Oh, you're here to see Addie." She laughed a bit more and added, "Yeah, that Addie's a busy lady, but she'll be with you in just a moment." She asked us to take a seat and said that someone would be right with us. A few minutes passed, and she looked up and said, "Can I ask what you needed?"

We both smiled, and I know we were both thinking the same thing. *Helloooo? We're at a tax office. We are here for taxes. What else could we be here for?* But instead, we opted to hand her my tax papers. "I needed my taxes done as per the appointment with Addie," I explained.

With that said, she looked over the papers and said, "Oh, this is a business. I don't do businesses taxes. Did my card say that? My card doesn't say I do businesses, does it? I'm Addie!" Too funny. I guess Addie *was* a busy woman! So if you're confused don't be; I was too. *This* was Addie and she *was* busy. Too funny.

We just smiled as we listened to Addie go on about not being able to do my taxes. "You know what?" she said. "I think Gerry does this type of taxes, so I will ask him." With that, she left and came back a few minutes later. "He can't do it, but someone else will be right out, and she is the best in our office. She does this type of taxes."

We sat for a few minutes longer, and then our new and third tax agent appeared. I was amused, because I kept saying to Elia, "We will get whom spirit knows we need to be with." I must have said that about six times.

Now standing before us was a new, very somber woman. It's not that she was being mean or anything; she was just somber, to the point, and not the kind of gal who was jumping with joy at work. I kept thinking, *I can work with this, I can work with this.*

The woman looked over my papers and said very slowly, "So... what do you want me to do with this?"

Well, I need you to do my taxes. I replied, "I was told to bring this stuff to you, and you would do my taxes."

She then slowly asked me, "So... you want me to file these?"

I felt so puzzled and said to her, "Well, yes." I chuckled.

She looked at me confused yet emotionless and, again, slowly said, "Well... these have already been filed by your business partner... and so to do this again, I would have to have all the documents to start again."

Boy, I really was getting confused, as I was only doing what I had been advised to do, and the advice given to me was apparently incorrect. I and this woman were not only, not on the same page, but we were not even in the same volume in the same library; we were states away.

All of a sudden my wife tries to clarify adding, "He has all of the information you keep saying he needs on all of the other forms he brought."

We knew what we wanted, so we just needed somehow to get our thoughts connected. She looked and all of a sudden said, "Oh, I see. You just need your taxes done."

I wanted to whack myself in the head. *Really?* I thought. *You just got that? Taxes done in a tax office—yep, that's me. I want my taxes done.* I started to chuckle as I thought, *Wasn't that the same thing I had been saying the last fifteen times?* Instead, I smiled and said to her, "Awesome. Yes, I just need my taxes done."

With that said, she looked at me, still not smiling, and said, "Well, Addie can do that for you. I don't do this type of taxes. She does."

Oh my! I just wanted to whack myself once again. Really? I just talked to Addie when I walked in. A tax office and no one can do my taxes, because that's not what they specialize in? Okay, whatever, right. I smiled and looked at her and said, "Okay."

She walked away, saying, "Let me go and get Addie, and she will help finish up your taxes with you."

A few moments later, she walked back into the room and said, "Well, I am not sure where Addie went to, but if you have a seat, she will be back soon, I am sure."

My wife said to her, "I think I saw her go to lunch."

Don't feel confused. Keep reading.

Great, I thought. *How long is lunch?* But then it would be okay, as I had all day, and I knew that I really needed my taxes done. I could wait. The lady then turned to my wife and said, "Didn't you say you already filed your taxes?"

My wife said, "Yes, I already did."

She then said to my wife, "May I ask why you didn't file taxes together?"

Elia then so proudly said to her, "Well, you see, I am transgender, and the federal government doesn't honor us as a married couple."

I tell you, what happened next was so beautiful. This somber-looking woman lit up with a smile like the fourth of July and said, "*No!* No way! I would have never known! I would have never guessed! You are so *stunning*; you are so beautiful! You go, girl! You look *amazing*, and I would *never* have guessed!" Then she added, "You know what? I am not sure where Addie is, but I can take care of you myself."

The rest of the time with our new tax agent, Mary Ann, was heavenly. We talked of the medium work that we do and how awesome she thought that was. She told us of her personal religion but was so thrilled and honored by what we did. We shared stories of her father who was now in spirit and how she felt his energy brush by her when he crossed over into death as she knew it. We shared how wonderful it is for us to be able to touch others' hearts with words of healing from beyond the earth plane. And even got my taxes done to boot! She stated that she was glad it was late in the tax season so we were able to have the time to chat longer and share stories as we had done.

It had been a treasure in meeting her, as we felt so at home with this lovely woman. She now had a smile that would just not quit. Elia and I were thrilled. We had such a good time that when we were done, she had forgotten to bring out our papers for us. It was fun hearing her say, "Oh my goodness, I left your papers back in my office. Hang on, and I will just go back and get them." I think the best part was yet to come.

I am such a believer in karma and the ripple in your pond and passing out random acts of kindness. I have always believed that goodness begets goodness.

By the time we had finally all made it to the front desk to pay for our taxes, Addie was back and able to cash us out. To our left, this young couple had just walked in and stepped up to the counter. Our tax agent, Mary Ann, was now truly "Merry" Ann. She was somber as a judge an hour before and now was beaming with a smile and greeting with a bright, cheerful heart. My heart was touched to see that a change had taken place. A ripple was happening because we had connected. I knew as she waved to us as we left that we would be greeted the next time when we returned to have our taxes done once again.

I knew she would be smiling for the rest of the day. I and Elia left and looked inside the front window only to see Merry Ann waving with cheer and continuing on with her new clients. What a great day it had been. *Funny*, I thought. *We only went to have the taxes done, but we watched someone named Mary transform into Merry.*

Love is always the
key to happiness.

Love,

Emmanuel

EMMANUEL, YOU NEED TO LEARN TO LOVE

*I*t was an awesome week with five of the top mediums of the world. I and Elia were so blessed to have been part of such a wondrous week of learning. We were complimented on how beautiful and loving we were, and I was grateful that I was able to hear those words, as it was confirmation that we were doing what we love to do—*love.*

Matter of fact, it was at the beginning of the week when one of the teachers wanted to do a demonstration to show how strong love is from spirit yet how sometimes at the same time mediums can get the wrong connection. She explained that the demonstration was hard to do because it's hard to find two people in a class who are so closely bonded with love that they are almost one. I and Elia were so blessed when she said, "However, we are blessed to have such a love with us this week with the love of Emmanuel and Elia."

Our teacher demonstrated, and I and Elia loved being a lesson of love for all to see. We do our best to have fun everywhere we go. I have to say Elia is my one and my one true love. The thought of being without her brings me to tears. She is the ba to the boom of my heart, and she feels the same about me. We know that we are blessed to have found each other in this life.

With both of us being married before, our marriages were agonizing, but they were the lessons we chose and the people we chose to be with to learn the lessons. I can also say that we were blessed to have been with our former spouses and yet are blessed to have been able to divorce and find each other. I know we finally breathe and feel that to walk with the other is to always walk in sunshine and love. Not everyone in our past approved or supported us, but who cares? We approve, and that is all that matters to us—our love. As I am writing this, I and Elia have been together eight years. We never argue. We never fight, as we have a motto, "When you truly love someone, what is there to argue about?" We both wake each day eager to see the face of the other. I have days when I will sit all day crying because of our love and how beautiful she is to me.

It was now the end of the week, and it was time to get ready to leave and return to our home in Boston. Tears were falling, as we both knew that some of the people we'd met we would see again and some we would not. But no matter, we knew eventually in spirit we would actually see them all. The sun was shining, and our trip home would be lovely, so we bid our farewells and left the building to walk up the pathway that led to our cabin. It was time to pick up our luggage.

We were almost in sight of our cabin when someone stopped us to say good-bye. A few more tears fell as they thanked us for our radiant love. They started to leave when another person stopped by to give us their business card so we could keep in touch. A few more tears fell as we heard yet another time, "Thank you for the love that we all felt from you. Thank you for working with us, as we were honored to feel the presence of your love."

I and Elia were in awe of the love being given back to us. Personally, we felt honored that the universe gave us the privilege to have been able to be with so many loving teachers and students alike. I looked up and wiped the tears, and smiled as this lovely woman who had been a student in our classroom that week started to pass by.

I smiled to her and said, "Hello. You are so beautiful."

With that, she started walking toward me with her smile and her head tipped to the side.

I said to her, "You just remind me of my sister."

Although this woman was about five eleven, and my sister was about a foot shorter, she carried a similar energy about her. She inquired about my sister. Though I knew better than to give her any information, I ignored my higher voice inside and let a few parts come out. I told her that although I love my sister, we hadn't seen each other or spoken in a few years because she wanted to direct my life instead of respecting my life. I added that although I love her, she was very judgmental in her ways and wasn't interested in chatting, just dictating to me what I should do and telling me that I was going to hell because I was spiritual and not religious.

Now haven't we all had days when we have thought to ourselves, *I have been in a spiritual retreat for a week now. I should be able to just speak freely by the end of the week without being slapped down because I was just feeling it in the moment.* What was I thinking?

Within an instant, this lovely young lady was telling me that I needed to learn to be more loving and that I really needed to learn how to be forgiving. Guess who wished he could have backpedaled in that moment? Right... Well, it got even better as I said to her, "Oh, I think you misunderstood. I adore my sister. She just believes I should be attending her church and asking her for forgiveness for what I don't know and ... and ... and ... but I love her."

With that said, here it came again, "Well, it sounds like you have some issues you need to deal with concerning love. I think you really just need to learn how to love."

Okay, so right in that moment I actually chuckled, right out loud, "*Really?*"

"Really," she answered.

I really had to laugh out loud. I knew this conversation was going to go nowhere. She had no idea the history and the years I had spent doing my best to love my family while they chose to abuse, all the while I chose to continue to love them. Love wasn't enough, and I wanted to live. Funny how sometimes it's just best to smile and say, "You remind me of someone I love," and leave it at that. So I decided that I needed to just let it go and move on, but this lovely young lady—well... shall we say...had an agenda of "saving" me.

I smiled and thought to myself, *You really do remind me of my sister. She wanted to save me too, but I needed no saving.* But, I only wanted to share the love, so I did my best and said, "You know, I love my sister. We just don't see eye to eye."

The young lady quickly replied in such a sweet voice with eyes squinted, head tipped, and towering over me, "See, Emmanuel," she spoke in such a patronizing tone, "you have a problem loving and forgiving. When you learn to love and be forgiving—"

I tell you what—my eyebrows were raised up to my forehead. My eyes were huge, and I started chuckling again. "Really?" I asked. "*Really?*"

She smiled with her head tipped and said *so* seriously, "Really."

I took a deep breath (as I knew that was the only way I was going to get in another word) and said, "Were you *in* the same class as I was this week? I mean, did you *hear* Elia this week during class? Did you *miss* us at the front of the room for the *love* lesson?" Yep, I really knew I needed to find a gracious way to move on and move this young lady on too.

She continued to give me her agenda, as I smiled and said, "I need you to do me a favor." I got very quiet and said, "I need you to take those two beautiful lips that you have and close them." I smiled and said to her in a very gentle voice, "Okay now, come on. Come on, *you can do it.* Just close them."

She took a breath and said, "But you—"

"No, no. No more. I just need you to listen now and close those beautiful lips." Again, I said sweetly, yet patronizingly, "Come on. I know you can do it."

She started in yet again, and I cut her off, "Nope, no more. Come on now. I know that you can do this. Come on. Just put 'em together."

She finally listened, and as she put her lips together, I said, "Now that's better, and now I want you to bend your head down so I can reach your forehead with my lips, so I can kiss your forehead."

She leaned down, and I kissed her forehead. I told her I loved her and instantly said, "Okay. Now you can go. Go on now, be on your way—shoo, shoo now. Be off—bye, bye."

With that, she was off, and Elia was standing there watching me with a few others with big eyes, grins, and looks of "What on earth was she doing?!" I know I felt as if the Dali Lama had just been kicked in the groin because a student didn't think he was peaceful enough. Funny how some can't even see the sun shining on a clear summer's day when that's the only thing in the sky above.

For those who can see, I say, "I love you." And for those who cannot see, I say, "I love you too." We *all* need love, no matter what. You know that statement "Judge not, as ye be judged"? So often people want to just slam you in the name of their own righteousness. Don't be like that. Know that being loving is better. Know that you haven't walked in their shoes, so don't slap them down. Maybe they just wanted to share a bit of their story freely without being beat down for their honesty. We all like to share, so the next time someone shares with you, maybe you should just listen and be kind and loving instead of being their judge and jury.

I fell in love the day
my eyes saw you

Love,
Emmanuel

CHOICES

*T*hough she doesn't talk, at least she is still alive today living her dreams.

So many of us are afraid to share heartache because we feel, how can that be inspirational when a part of us feels we have lost something? Funny, though, in the lessons of life, heartache brings great outcomes of great growth. When one chooses to see the depth of love, they can then understand there was no heartache at all, just a lesson to be learned.

For many years, I have been asked if I would write a story about how to raise the perfect child. I always smile and say, "Well, that is easy. Love your child as much as possible, and if they ever choose to walk away, know you did the best you could and love them still."

It was about eight or so years ago when my daughter JC went to college. I had always been the stay-at-home parent. My first wife and I made a joint decision I was going to stay home and raise the family. *I* would stay home and raise the children, as we didn't want to hire a babysitter to give our children babysitter values. Instead, we wanted one of us to stay home and give them what *we* felt was loving—*our* values.

I had always hoped that my children would grow up to be strong. If they so chose, they would be able to move as far away as they wanted because of the strength that I had given them. My wife at the time didn't want to give up her career and felt she didn't have very nurturing qualities to raise children. I was good with that, as I loved the thought of being a parent. I knew it was going to be the hardest job ever but the most rewarding as well. I knew even in my youth that we are not born with a manual in our diaper. Its called, do the best you can with what you have. I have always believed that in the universe there are no mistakes, just lessons to learn. Just my opinion, as it works for me.

One of my daughters had a moment with a family member in her childhood that I never knew about until her teens. It took some time for me to deal with the issue. As a parent, the thought that I should have known would ring in my ears for some time. I should have protected my daughter from that predator. As I healed through it, I realized the moment happened, and I was not to blame. I grew and moved on. However, my daughter never moved beyond it. She found comfort in blame and began cutting herself. It would be a roller coaster ride with her for many years.

It was the beginning of her second year in college when I would get the call to come and pick her up, as they were booting my daughter out of college. I was so confused and felt so alone as my wife at that time wanted me to just ignore it, because that would make it go away. I knew that was not the case, but getting our daughter help would be the best thing possible. I drove three hours with a friend to JC's college. I went with my close buddy Gerald because my daughter had tried to kill herself, and my wife was too busy to help out.

Off we went on our three-hour drive, and a bit more, to pick up my daughter. I had no details at this time, as the college just said she must leave that night. So, I was on my way. I arrived to JC's dorm room to find a group of girls. They introduced themselves as her "best friends."

"We have been doing our best watching over JC each time she has tried to kill herself," they said.

My eyes widened.

"We watched over," they said, "so as not to let her go too far."

I stood bewildered at what I was hearing. I kept thinking *what kind of friend watches you kill yourself*? I was in shock by the words I was hearing. I was taken in to an office where the dean of the school let me know that on numerous occasions my daughter had slit her wrists while attempting to end her existence.

The dean wanted me to know that JC needed mental help and went on to say that she needed to be admitted to a hospital. JC had already agreed to check herself in. I would need to take her to our home hospital. My head was spinning, as I kept thinking, *I did the best I could, and that wasn't good enough. . ., what did I do?*

It took a bit, but in time I saw that I did do the best I could, as JC's choices were hers and not mine. I was not to blame for her choices. I had been raised in a rather abusive environment, but she had not. She was raised with love. I had been there. I wouldn't find out till many years later that there was an abuser in the home, but it wasn't me. I would find out in later years that each time I would leave the home, their mother would tell them, "You can *never* talk to your father. He'll *never* listen. You can *never* ask him *anything*." She scolded them, "One day I am going to leave that —— (you get the picture) and when I do, you had better be ready to choose, and the choice you make had *better be me*."

"You can *never* talk to your father, he won't listen," was quite a statement—what a lie.

The day my son told me that statement and the others confirmed that she had said those things, I cried for days wondering *what I had ever done to her besides love her?* It matters not, as she still needs and deserves love too. We all do, no matter what. With that said, I and my buddy drove JC to the hospital. It would take a lot of days in the ward for my daughter before she could come home. She was told she could never return to the college, as filled with rage she had held a pair of scissors to another student's throat, so she was banned from ever returning—at least that was what we were told.

Now this is for all who have ever done the best you could, and it just wasn't good enough. This is for those who never understood that maybe something else, maybe something that you didn't know, was going on, as was the case with me at that time. People would always say to I and my wife, "You have the best children." "You have the most polite children." I would smile along with my wife and say thanks.

It was beautiful to see that others could see the children's beauty shining through, but now I was on another side of a building that I never knew existed, and I couldn't find my way back to the other side. I can remember when JC was in the hospital ward, and I walked onto the floor as everyone in the room had their eyes fixed on me. It was a rather creepy feeling, but what got worse was when I asked what was going on and found out that they all felt my daughter harmed herself because of me.

Wow! My world was spinning, and it felt like someone wanted to take me down.

Eventually, my daughter came home. One night she got mad because she couldn't have her way, so she waited for us all to get to our porch swing. Then, just before we were to go to bed, she announced with a tear filled whine that while we were sleeping, she was going to kill herself. *Oh dear God in the universe, not again*, I thought. The other children just looked at her.

I remember saying, "JC, you do know that I now have to take you back to the hospital where either you can check yourself in, or I will check you back in. But one way or the other, you will have to go back. You need help, and I cannot help you." Ignoring her and going to bed would not be loving. For me being loving meant that I cared. I would *have* to take her to the hospital.

She wasn't happy, and I didn't care that she needed someone to blame again. I let her know that if she needed someone to blame, I had had big shoulders and could take it. All I knew was she needed love and a hospital bed to keep her safe. I asked my oldest at the time to keep watch of the others, and off I went once again to the hospital to have JC admit herself into the ward.

Sometimes the best thing we can do for our children is to just let go.

I needed to let go. I didn't know at the time why my children wouldn't talk to me. I just knew they wouldn't, and each time I would say, "You know you can talk to me," they would just clam up and say nothing at all. I didn't know at that time they had been threatened each day by my ex. I had no idea that each time I went out to do yard work, chores, or garden work or when I would just go outside for a bit of air, my children were being threatened.

Life at that time was hard, living with the not knowing. It would be many years later, my daughter would completely stop talking to me but not before she told me, "My mother was *right*. We can *never* talk to you. You will *never* listen to us, so why bother?" She stopped talking after telling me that she hoped I would die and rot in a hole. I could understand, as I remember after being strapped by my father, I wanted to punish him too.

Now this may sound like a "woe is me," but it is nothing of the sort. So many live in the silence of a sad truth that all is secretly kept quiet in their home while the dirty little secret is passed on to yet another generation. Many know they did the best they could do but never see it because they don't want anyone to think that they weren't a good person. I knew this beautiful man so many years ago. As a child, he would visit our home just to talk. His name was Art, and Art was a minister.

Not very many knew that when he went behind closed doors, his wife would hit him with pots and pans and her cane, beating him till her anger was gone. I remember the day he told my family the story. It was the day after his wife had taken ill and had become bedridden. You see, Art had showed up again with bruises, and this time he let us know why they were there. Before he would claim that he had fallen or was working outside and got hit by something in the barn—always an excuse. He needed help but never got it. Who could ever know the dirty little secret?

His wife never beat him again, as she grew weak from illness and age and finally died, giving Art peace. Now we both had some dirty little secrets. Help was needed, but everyone was blaming the man who had given his family loving support. I felt alone and in darkness without a light to see anything but myself, and so did Art. Our lights felt so dim. My life's purpose has always been to be loving and be the example we *all* want to be. Yet in that moment I felt like Art, battered behind the doors in secret. Maybe it was only with words, but I had to find a way to rise above the words of battering and realize *I* had the power *within me* to move beyond it all. To move beyond *all* the stress and glares, and know *I* had done the best *I could* do and am *still* doing the best *I can*. I have always loved helping others heal and find their journeys when they've felt lost, but here *I* was feeling lost.

My children had a lie battered in them, but it had been a secret that I was not to be told. There was a plan, and I knew nothing of it. My eldest would avoid me. My daughter decided to never talk to me again. Out of six children, now only four would talk and soon, another son would be yelling at me that I never listened to him. The same message kept being repeated till one by one each told me. Another would leave and move in with his sister, as he stopped talking to me.

Now I was in my kitchen asking the three left what I had done.

All stood silent.

Nothing but silence as they left the room with me in tears not understanding. It would be about two months of a lot of silence until one day my eldest saw me crying again. I asked him again what I had done. What had I ever done besides love all of them? He looked at me that day and said, ever so quietly, "Padre, I have never wanted to tell you. I have always been so afraid to say, but my whole life, every time you would go out the door to work or whatever, Momma would corner me and tell me that one day she was going to leave you. When the day came, I had better choose, and that choice would be her." He spoke with tears in his eyes. "Padre, Momma wanted us all to know that we could *never* trust you. She wanted us to know that we could never talk to our father, as you would only get angry and be mad at us. We just grew up believing what she had said."

Wow! I thought as I fell back against the wall. *Wow.* Another of my sons decided to stop being mad at me that day and said, "Padre, you have *never* done that. You have *always* loved us and talked to us and have *always* listened to *us*." He looked at me, hugged me, and said, "I am so sorry."

I remember looking at him and saying, "I am so sorry too, Honey. I never knew what you were told. I am so sorry."

My heart was so heavy with tears, wondering what I had ever done to their mother except love her, but I knew that sometimes it's not what we have done but what someone else has done. It's not what *we* can *give*, but what *others* can *receive*. It's *always* choice.

I learned a lot that day and learned to move on.

We were divorced, and she did have three who decided to believe that she was right and they could never talk to me. I flashed to a day when our son was married, and I wanted her to know I loved her. She wanted me to know I had a funny way of showing that, since I never ran after her.

I was confused, as *she* had left *me and the six children*. Sometimes you just have to count your blessings that you are alive and go beyond without blame. Life was what it was. It had love and drama, and now it had ended.

But I had to go on. I had made it an art in life—that word *love*. But love cannot fix unless it's the love *inside of you* that fixes what *you* believe needs fixing inside of *you*.

It's been years, and some of my children are still working through the healing of a misguided secret. Sometimes it can seem difficult to change a negative thing you have chosen believe, because it has become such a habit.

"Why bother to change?" my grandmother would say to me. "I am old and set in my ways. It's too late for me to change."

Not so.

It's *never* too late to change. I was raised to be something different than what I am because I *wanted* to change. But *I* made the choice. Was it work? Of course it was work, but some habits are not good for us. They're just very bad habits, and sometimes we just need to change them. "Everything in moderation," my son always says to me. I agree; too much of something is just too much.

Funny how years ago someone told me they were going to the store. Could they get me anything? I told them we needed tissues and asked if they would pick me up a few boxes, I would pay them when they got to my home. They arrived with *two cases* of tissues. They thought I could use a few extra. Just to let you know, I have had plenty of tissues for three years now. Too much, is just too much.

I am proud of all of my children. I am proud of how I raised them. I raised them to be loving, kind, and strong. I raised them to believe that if they wanted to go to Timbuktu, Africa, they would have the strength to do just that. I raised a valedictorian and a salutatorian. I raised four others to believe they were just as smart as the rest. So to me, I have success, whether they want to believe a lie or not. I know my daughter is alive today because she had a father who cared enough to *say* he cared and did his best to show it. I can smile and say I know children who choose not to talk, shouldn't be punished but loved instead. As I have always believed, the best gift you can ever give your child is their freedom.

I know I wanted a life of my own, and I have it. I wanted to have a partner who just wanted to love me like I would love myself; and I have that too.

Sometimes we feel that just because it didn't turn out the way we wanted it to, something was wrong. That's just not so at all. Maybe we were just the vessel of love to bring students to a planet of lessons. Maybe the students just had an agenda for their lives, and it didn't include you. For me, I can be good with that and still love them, because all need love.

For all who have all of their children with them for every holiday and every day's event, bless you. But remember we are all not alike, and we all do have our own lives to live. I am so proud of all of my children for living what they choose in life, even if that means I am not included in it. I wanted a life, and I have it—my own. Funny thing, I can thank my children for giving that to me—a life. I grew up.

"It's okay to be the daisy
in a field of roses."

Love,
Emmanuel

JUST BE REAL

It's so funny for me to hear my children say, "Padre, you are so eccentric." For years I was a bit puzzled, as I was only being me, and to be me, was just what it is. I would say that to my children, and they would say with a chuckle, "And yes, that's you."

Then I would say, "I just don't get it."

To which they would add, "That's because you are who you are, and that's eccentric." They would then try their best to explain. They would begin with, "Well, look how you dress."

And I would say confused, "What's wrong with the way I dress? I like it."

To which they would add with a smile, "But, Padre, *no one* dresses like you."

I would smile and say to them, "Well, maybe people *should* dress more like me, and they would feel better and freer being themselves." Then I would say, "So how does that make me that word?" I mean, if you could have seen me at this time, quite matter-of-factly defending myself being me; and to me, that was enough.

I would sit with a grin on my face while they would say, "Padre, you wear jewelry."

"So? I see men wear jewelry all the time."

Their rebuttal was, "But, Padre, have you looked in the mirror lately? You wear it *everywhere*."

"So?"

Then I would get, "Padre, you wear makeup."

I would tell them, "So? I like what I wear on my eyes. It makes me feel better, and I like how it makes me look."

Again, they would say, "Padre, you're a bit eccentric." I felt I was still just being me, and to me, that's just me. They began again with, "Padre, who paints their ceiling like the Sistine Chapel? Who paints all of their house trim gold? Who puts statues and chandeliers throughout their home?"

I smiled at them and said, "Well... that would be me." To which they would add, "Padre, that's eccentric." I smiled at them and finally said, "If eccentric is being me, then I will say it must be an amazing thing to be eccentric, because I love being me."

I love seeing the lights shine bright and sparkles, like a rainbow from the heavens. I love wearing gold on my eyes, because it makes *me* feel good. I love seeing paintings on the ceiling, because when I'm looking up, I want to see beauty, too. I love wearing jewelry and feeling fun. I love being me and letting what's inside shine on the outside. So for me, I know that to be real, you just have to be who you are. For me, to shine is to just be me. I have always known that it's always best to be who you are and not to try to be someone else. That's too hard of a job. But to be me is to wake every day and do my best to shine what's inside out.

I can remember so many years ago as a child. My childhood was filled with dreams even on an extremely poor farm. I was one out of six children. I was the next to the youngest. Sometimes there was barely enough for all of us to eat, but we always had enough and we were always fed and clean. Yes, my life had its ups and downs. I was born into the era of "spare the rod, spoil the child." I could have lived without the rod, the stick, the switch, the fly swatter, the belt, *and* the hand. I think you get the drift... But life just was what it was, and blaming people will never get me anything but a life filled with sorrows and blame.

The past was just the book my parents came into this life with—*their* lessons, *their* past. I remember snow flying in my room in the wintertime because our home was so poor, but that didn't mean I didn't get love. To me, the snow in my room was a magical wonderland, and I stared in its show of glittery life. Snow on my bed in the wintertime is one of my best childhood memories—just me and the snow. I loved how it sparkled in the moonlight. I always had plenty of wool blankets to keep me warm. I got the best my parents knew how to give at that time. But best of all, I did have that magic *inside of me*, that magic that was waiting to come out to blossom and bloom and become the color-filled canvas that I am.

I remember one day having the need to feel what it would be like to be homeless and opted to live on the streets. I ate where I could find food. I washed in a creek and used water fountains for drink. My life was what I wanted it to be—*mine*. It would be quite an adventure until I would eventually find residence in a home and find love in another way.

I remember vividly the day I married and had children of my own and did the best I could for them and my wife. Still, I was painting my canvas the way I wanted me to look. I went from brown hair to red hair, then red hair to white hair. I grew long hair, and then one day, I shaved it bald just to see how it felt for me to be me. I loved it and still smile remembering that the person then is this person now—just better.

I remember making my own clothes, as well as my wife's and children's clothing then. I loved the abilities I had chosen to explore. My canvas of colors was growing and spreading, as I grew gardens of flowers and vegetables *everywhere*. I was showing my children that to be free, it was okay to grow up and be who they would choose to be, and I was free to be me.

It would be many years, and I would eventually be divorced, as my wife of that time needed a new canvas to look at. We were both so blessed to have moved on to find love again in other places. Not all of my children chose to stay connected to me, and that was okay too. As they all told me, I was eccentric, and I guess emotionally I am too. I chose to be happy, because I too wanted my life to be a canvas for me to paint. They would all also choose to paint their canvases the way they chose them to look.

I have heard it said so many times that in life, you never know what you're going to get. But for me, I have always felt that life is what you choose to make it, and that's every moment of every day. In other words, I can choose to see bad in everything, or I can choose to see that there is *always* good in *everything*. Life really is a choice, and I have found that eccentric is not a bad choice if I want to be eccentric. It just is what it is. Life is beautiful, and I am glad I have made the choices I have in life. It has been fulfilling thus far, and I plan on continuing that fulfillment of my heart.

I tell people, "If it works, work it, and if not, let it go." I have never liked spinning my wheels in a rut.

So what's my point?

Well, we can all sit around complaining and whining, or we can move on and shine our lights for all to see. Personally, to shine makes me feel good. To let others live the lives they choose feels good to me. But the best is to influence a heart to shine and shine to its fullest potential. The best is seeing the truth for what it was and then letting go and letting God and not the ego take charge. The best is planting the seed and nurturing it, so it can grow and change into magnificent beauty.

My children? Well, they're off doing what they need to do, what makes them happy.

My wife now? Well, she just loves to watch me create and inspire and grow. She's awesome.

And me? Well, I guess I finally embraced that eccentric thing and decided to make the word as beautiful as I feel I am.

One, can always make
a difference.

Love,
Emmanuel

THE BRACELET

I sit here in my home, and I think to myself, *Emmanuel, you are so blessed.*

My life has been filled with so many tragedies and pain, yet the only thing I feel is how blessed I am to have lived the life I have. I have known homelessness; I have known what it is like to go hungry. I have known the emotional pain that comes with having more bills than money and asking why and why me. I have known the loss of death of loved ones and myself personally. I have known the loss of losing a child to death and losing children to life. I have. And yet still, the only thing I can feel is blessed to be living the life I live.

I remember as a child, feeling my sister hold me as my family traveled to the west. As I recall, I was about five or six years of age. My mother's family lived out west, so all seven of us would pack into the car, with the trunk filled with luggage, and off we would go. My dad would drive straight through, as we never had the extra money to stop and stay in a motel. That was just the way it was.

Some of us forget that our parents kept those secrets to themselves so their children would never feel poor. I know I never told my children we were poor even when we lived in a trailer and never had enough money to pay all the bills. We managed it with six children of our own, and it wasn't always an easy day. We were told we lived below the poverty level, but I never knew it, and neither did my children. We thought we were the richest ever—kings, and queens, princes and princesses. I knew with the love we had, we were.

I can remember so beautifully how it felt traveling in the arms of my sister. I can remember how she loved me then. What a beautiful feeling I still have from the memory as tears fall from my eyes as I remember. I can remember saying to my siblings as a child, "One day I am going to have enough money that I will be able to buy you an elephant." I loved elephants and always felt they were such a noble creature. Was it nobility I wanted to give them?

Well, it actually wasn't till yesterday when a friend named Priscilla gave Elia and I an elephant that I recalled the memory. As the memory goes, in my midtwenties I would marry, and I would get to help my sister who lovingly held me as a child. Now mind you, she had her gnarly moments, but this moment was not one of them. I remember going to her home where she and her husband had a few children of their own. I remember loving their children and wishing they were mine. I couldn't wait to be a dad.

I also remember hearing them arguing about where they were going to get enough groceries to survive and how they were going to buy the diapers they needed for their babes. My heart ached for them. I knew how it felt, but I and my wife were starting out at that time, and we barely had enough as it was. But I know we have all had these moments when you just know you need to help someone, no matter what, and just trust that it will be fine.

So that night, I left my sister's home with such a heavy heart. I said to my wife, "Let's help them. Let's go to the store and buy some groceries, diapers, and a few treats for the children and take them over in the middle of the night." I asked my wife, "Can we do this, you and I? Can we do this even though I know we don't have a lot ourselves?" She looked at me like I was absolutely insane, but agreed.

Off we were to the grocery store with a list in hand of all of the foods they needed and some special treats as well. I remember feeling higher than a kite could fly. My wife at that time just went along with the flow of things. She always felt I was a bit insane and too giving, yet I knew we had to do what was needed, and that was to take care of something that was extremely important. Someone had a need much greater than ours.

The next thing was to cash out, knowing that we would be living on what we had. But I knew that we were and always had been taken care of, and I trusted that. I had always hoped that my wife then could have seen that when we trust, all will be well—it always is. We took the groceries home and got everything all ready for delivery, but I wanted to make sure they didn't know who had delivered the goods. We would wait till about three in the morning before we left our home. We would then travel about twenty minutes away to deliver the groceries.

Ah, delivery time was awesome. It was that feeling of doing something so special for someone who needed what you could offer. We made sure to get everything quietly on their front porch. I made sure that the special treats for the children—bananas, peanut butter, Oreos, and a bag of candy goodies—were able to be seen. I knew the children's favorite things and wanted them to feel the joy too, not just Mom and Dad. I feel we both left that night feeling very special inside. I know I feel that specialness inside even today.

I know that sometimes in life we all just need to do what we feel we need to do, even when others say you're absolutely nuts. If you're harming no one and giving love and helping another soul, what's so wrong or nuts about that? You know what? I have heard that for years, and I know I am *not nuts*. I know I am love. I know I am blessed for what I do and have done in life. I know that sometimes life looks as if it is dishing us out a bad rap, but it's not. We are, and when we finally stop all of the whys, we become the wise and see what's clearly in front of us.

It was last week when my lovely Elia and I were with a very large group of students. We went to learn and to teach as well. While we were there,

I decided to wear a stunning bracelet. I'd had this crystal piece of jewelry for some time and absolutely adored its beautiful color. It was a soft yellow. It reminded me of my baby sister's hair: golden sunshine. My baby sister had died of cancer when I was a child, and now as a medium, I am able to continue to know her and connect with her on an amazing new level.

Well, I had bought the bracelet many months prior but had never worn it. Usually, I would look at it and think, I just wasn't wearing the right color for it, so I would just leave it in its box. Elia would encourage me to wear it, but I would tell her I was just going to continue to charge it with my love until I was ready. So, this was the day I had finally chosen to wear it, and I was the only one who had touched it.

Every day I would look at the bracelet with love and ask the universe to put my love into it. It would be such a joy to find that the creator of the bracelet was inside the building where we were with her tables set up, selling all of her beautiful line of jewelry.

We would all be in the same place for class where the jewelry was also set up at the back of the room to be sold. Class would be amazing, and then it would be time for everyone to see the jewelry collection and purchase one or many if they chose. All the pieces were and are charged with energies and love to give them a powerful intention. I loved them, and that was my intention, as I love to sparkle and shine and that is exactly what this jewelry does.

There were so many looking at the sparkle and shine that I and Elia decided that we would look a bit later and go off for lunch. We walked out of the building and started up the path when this young lady came up to me and said, "Hi, my name is Karen. I just wanted to tell you I love your presence and how you both look. You are both so beautiful." She added, "Did you get to see the bracelets? They are so beautiful."

We both smiled and told her that we had and then showed her what we were wearing. Karen looked at us and said, "You know what? I tried on a few, and the energy is so powerful on them all, but I couldn't find one that felt comfortable on me. I am going to go back later and talk to the lady who makes them, so I can find one that harmonizes with me. They felt good but almost hurt when I had them on, but I really, really want one. I just need to find one that's more loving to me I guess."

I smiled to her and knew why I had worn my bracelet. I remember saying to my beautiful Elia, "I am not sure if this is actually mine, but I will just continue to give it my love until its owner crosses my path or I finally feel it belongs to me."

I smiled to Karen and said, "Karen, try this on and see how it feels. See if this one bothers you."

She looked at me as I handed it to her and said, "Really? Can I touch it?"

I smiled and said, "Absolutely," as I placed it in her hand.

She held it in her hand and said, "Wow, the energy in this is so beautiful." As she spoke, tears filled her eyes. She looked at me and said, "Can I ask what the name of this bracelet is?"

I said, "Of course, it's called *my love*." At the same time, I and Elia said the same words: "Try it on."

Karen was so sweet as she said, "Are you sure? This is yours."

I assured her it would be fine. As she slipped it on, she said, "Wow, I will have to go back and get this one. The energy of this one is absolutely perfect." As her eyes were sparkling, she said once again, "What was the name of this bracelet?"

I said again, "My love." She looked at me, and I said to her, "Please leave it on. It belongs to you. It's yours—please enjoy my love."

With tears bursting from her eyes, she said, "Oh no. No."

At that point, I was looking at her with tears in my eyes and said, "Yes, Karen, it is yours. *Now feel my love.*"

She burst into tears and just sobbed as we stood with her. She couldn't talk, yet thanks and gratitude filled the air as she expressed her thanks with her tears and blessed bows of her head as an honor to us. I know I and Elia were and are so blessed to have shared that moment in time with Karen.

She wanted us to know that we would never know how important of a gift that was for her. I know for me, my life is a better life because I followed my heart in giving something that was so beautiful and needed to be given. What an honor my life has been to share the love of the heart with so many. What is a bracelet to give, especially when you cannot take it with you? Death has no luggage for jewelry.

I have always thought that if I died in some accident and my heart was given to someone, I would wish that it could be given to someone who was mean and angry and never knew love. I know that if they had my heart, they would know love, they would know tears, they would know forgiving and forgiveness, and *they* would know the gift it is to care and give to others.

As a child growing up, most of my childhood treasures were stolen from me. Some of my siblings felt that what was mine was theirs to take. I feel that was the past behind me, and I guess they needed it more than I. So much better to give than steal from another, and sometimes you just have to let go of what you will never get back. I know I am better for it in just letting it go where it needed to go. My life is so much better now, as I embrace the life I choose in being loving and giving. After all, what we give out always returns—you know, like planting a seed and then nurturing it. All of a sudden, you have a field of flowers, and all you did was give out one small seed.

I will never forget the loving arms that held me, no matter what changed as my sister grew in her life. I knew the love. I will never forget that my parents loved me even when their book of life said to obey or get strapped. That's all they knew, and it was just the time. I will never forget the day I was homeless and the world truly became my home. I will always remember the day the universe gave back to me and my life changed yet again. But this time, I would be able to have not only one bracelet, but I would be able to have a hundred if I chose. I will never forget the day I said thank you when someone accepted my love in a bracelet.

"If I could turn back the hands of time, I would change nothing."

Love,
Emmanuel

BRING FORTH YOUR LIGHT

*W*hile I and Elia were at the mall, this man kept staring at me. After about five minutes or so, he walked over to my side, stood next to the counter right next to us, looked up at me, and said, "Has anyone ever asked you if they could just take your picture? Do you do this professionally, because you just look so picture perfect?" Then he added, "You don't see couples like you nowadays."

With that said, I smiled and said to him, "Well, actually everywhere we go, someone does ask that question." Elia was beaming with awesomeness, and I smiled and said, "Absolutely you may take your photo if you would like."

We stepped to the side of the counter and held each other. We smiled the smile we love to share. He took the picture and apologized to us that the colors weren't as perfect or as beautiful as we were in person. How sweet. He told us once again how wonderful it was to meet us and to have been able to take our photo. He wanted it just for him to have.

"So beautiful," he stated. And with that said, he put away his camera, shook our hands, thanked us again, and was out the door as happy as happy could be.

Our son was with us and said, "Wow, Padre, that was awesome.

He saw how bright your lights were, and he wanted to capture what he felt."

We were moved and in awe that our son had noticed. I love being a beacon of light. I love being married to an awesome beacon of light as well. We are blessed. I am so filled with gratitude to be who I am.

I always smile when I hear people say to me, "You are so inspirational." I guess for me, I know no other way to be. I guess some could say I have quite an ego, but I don't believe that *ever*.

For me growing up, life was an awesome gift. Do I mean that my childhood was peaches and cream and filled with loving beings? Hmm ... that would be a yea—okay, *no*. The ego, I think, was beat out of me as a child. You weren't sure how you were supposed to feel most of the time. Believing you were more than what you thought you were was not an option I could talk about. So if there was an ego in the room, you knew it wasn't mine. So I am grateful in a way that I had what I had growing up. It keeps my head on straight continually.

I believe that we all choose our families before we come to the planet. I believe that we arrange in the spirit world the lessons we would like to learn. I know for me I've thought so many times in life, *What was I thinking, coming to a world filled with such turmoil?* And to top it all off, *why did I want to feel such abuse from a family I could call my own?* Such are the lessons we choose.

I think about it often and always come to the same conclusion. If you are beaten down, the only way left for you to go is up. If you want to get rid of the ego, being in my family growing up was the place. Your light is going out if that special thing you thought out loud was you. So to be special inside and out, you really had to feel it and keep it quiet. You had to hold it tenderly and appreciate the specialness that you knew you were, but inside and not out.

Once when one of my brothers ran away from home, I remember thinking, *What did I do?* I had always felt that. I adored him, and he only wanted to beat the crap out of me for existing. Imagine being a child getting hurt every corner you turned. It surely would make you stop and wonder what you did that was so bad that someone would want to hurt you every given breath of your day. For me, it didn't make me hate him. I felt compassion and love for him. I guess I loved him even more. As an adult, I am glad I did, because I know he needed love. Loving him didn't stop him from hitting me or humiliating me, though.

Whenever my brother had the opportunity, he would smack, hit, kick, or throw something at me just to hurt me—period. Yes, it hurt me. Yes, it upset me. But inside, I knew that it was right to love. I knew that I had him as a brother for a reason.

It would be a most saddened day, when I would hear my parents say that my brother had run away. My heart ached as I thought, *What must I have done to chase him away?* Even as a child, I knew I had always done my best to love him. As an adult, I am so amazed I was ever able to love him at all, because he was always casting his anger upon me in whatever form of abuse he could give.

I always remember the most wonderful gift—the words my mother gave me. Well, maybe not all of her words, but a few. My mother said to me one day as an adult, "They are afraid and were *always* afraid of your love." It took me awhile to digest that one, but when I did, I could finally see what they all had taught me—to love. I cried thinking that with all of the abuse I had received as a child, the only thing I could still think of was loving them.

Now let me stop here for a moment and tell you something. Does this all mean I want to have tea with them or dinners together? Does it all mean that I will be spending Christmas vacation with my family? Does it mean I long for birthday celebrations? That would be a *no*. Really.

I also know of a thing called reality checks. You can share with people who want to be shared with. But why walk into a place where you are not welcome? Just to prove that you can? Hmm, and what would that do? It would put me back into a fire that I chose to grow beyond. Just as I say marriage is not a contest, neither is family. I find that for me, families are the ones I am with, in the moment of now. Family means something different for all of us, so this is my version of life and my journey. It's not a bad life, as I became the most amazing being. I love, I love, and I love to *love*.

I have, again, some awesome teachers to thank. Were they loving to me then? I would have to say *not*. For me, it was what I took from life that helped me the most. It wasn't the blame, as anger was their lesson to feel; *their* lessons. I was touched by it, yet it just didn't stay. I had anger but finally let it go where it needed to go—back to those who gave it and taught it to me. I thanked it for its lessons and told the anger that it could go back to where it came from. I will never forget the day I actually did just that, and I think that moment changed my life forever. The pain stopped. The heartaches stopped. The "why me?" stopped. And the thank you's poured out of me.

We are here on this planet to learn lessons in life. What have you learned in life so far? Are you blaming others because they have and you do not? I have been through that one. Let it go and be free to live in the love and light that you are.

Are you busy wanting a better life that you see others have? Have it, but have your life not theirs.

Are you arguing with your spouse or your partner? If so, ask yourself why. Are you wanting to change that person, or is it you who needs to change?

I know I and my wife never argue. We believe that arguing is not loving, and we feel that when you love someone for all that they are, there is never anything to complain about. Complaints begin with *we* want something different from them, than what they are giving.

Every night as a child I fell asleep in fear. Every day I would wake to fear. Every day I would live in fear. But one day I found the way to bring my light of love forth. That was the most wonderful gift I was ever able to give myself. That was the day I started to fall in love with me.

I think you should fall in love with yourself right now and see what happens. I think everyone should fall in love with themselves. Life would only change for the better. Then your love would be so great that when the ego wants to pop in, you would say, "Well, I have to have some of you to function, but the other part will have to go."

I know that e.g.o. is edging God out. I know that we are a wonderful part of the puzzle of God, so I want as much of my loving self present as much as possible. But back to my childhood—to have the ego beaten out of me turned out to be quite a blessing in disguise, I guess. I grew to instinctively tell a rearing ego to go away.

I live with and am love. I say to you all, bring forth the light that is in you. Bring forth the loving light of creation that you are in to the moment of now. As much as you can, feel that most amazing part that is your soul. Know that your soul is perfect in every way, and no matter what you have done in life, it was a lesson to learn by, a lesson to learn from, and a lesson to help you grow beyond.

Need to be forgiving? Just write a note or tell someone you are sorry as you bring forth the light of love. I will tell you, the more you bring forth the light of creation, and that is your light, the more you will begin to glow.

I and my Elia travel and learn. We travel and teach, but every time we meet a group of light workers for the first time, they will always say, "Wow, your light is so bright."

For me, it is a blessing to hear that I have continued to grow on my journey. I am so glad that life was never a competition for me. Competitions were what I was raised with. I thank spirit in the universe that I was able to be touched and blessed by my childhood lessons, because now I can shine brightly for all who wish to see without needing an ego to be pleased. The love that radiates in me is pleased.

Let that light that is in you shine forth and let *you* be pleased. Let the love inside of you shine out for all to see without judgments or competitions of whose light is brighter—yours or mine. Bring forth your light and let it touch all nations with all of their people. Let the world feel your love and light. You will only be blessed for it.

The best part is, it costs nothing to bring forth your light. It just takes a bit of mental adjustment. Do it. It's so easy. It's so wonderful. Don't do it for others. Do it for yourself.

Feel the love. Feel the power as you bring forth your light.

Always loving you,
Emmanuel

CPSIA information can be obtained at www.ICGtesting.com
Printed in the USA
LVOW11s0620181213

365864LV00002B/5/P

9 781452 561967